S0-AGZ-711

Sterling Service

"Extraordinary Recipes for Ordinary Cooks"

Published by the Dothan Service League

Illustrations
by
Lisa McGowan

Photography
by
Buford Fuqua

18th Century   Dutch Basket

Cover photo: Old English tea service with a water pot, coffee pot, waste bowl, tea pot, creamer and sugar on an English gallery tray

The Dothan Service League is an organization of committed volunteers, working to enhance and improve the quality of life of all Dothan, Alabama residents.

All proceeds from the sale of *Sterling Service* will be used to support community projects of the Dothan Service League.

Additional copies may be purchased by addressing:

Sterling Service
Dothan Service League
P.O. Box 223
Dothan, Alabama 36302

or by placing credit card telephone orders:
1-334-671-7142

Copyright © 1996
Dothan Service League
Dothan, Alabama
ALL RIGHTS RESERVED

ISBN 0-9653997-0-2
Dothan Service League

Library of Congress Catalog Card Number: 96-71079

First Printing • October 1996 • 10,000 copies
Second Printing • September 2003 • 2,500 copies

WIMMER
COOKBOOKS

ConsolidatedGraphics

1-800-548-2537

Introduction

This cookbook has been published to honor the fifty years of truly *Sterling Service* given to our community by the members of the Dothan Service League of Dothan, Alabama. In this sense, we are defining sterling as something thoroughly excellent and of lasting quality, as is sterling silver.

As we know, presentation has a great deal to do with how food tastes. So, along with our more than 350 triple-tested recipes, we are featuring some heirloom silver pieces that belong to our families and including some hints on silver and linen care.

We have taken some liberties with our identification of silver pieces. For example, "dressing spoon with shell bowl" may not be the original name given this spoon, as old services could include hundreds of pieces, but if Grandma always called it her dressing spoon, then dressing spoon it is. Also, remember that most services had, for example, at least three different types of soup spoons. Here we merely say soup spoons. We find that using pieces in different ways can be refreshing!

Some of the silver pieces pictured can be identified as to date and maker, while others cannot. We hope that you will understand and appreciate our efforts, and find this cookbook to be a beautiful addition to your *Sterling Service*.

1899 Cup, minus Glass Liner,
by Peter Karl Fabergé
of St. Petersburg, Russia

Cookbook Committee

Cookbook Reprint Chairmen
Juanita Sykes & Pam Pitman
2003-04

Cookbook Chairmen
Robin Brookshire & Cindy Hollis
1996-97

Rosemary McKibben	Janet Marsella	Terri Turner
1995-96	1994-95	1993-94

Creative Director/Managing Editor
Audrey Miller

Recipe Editing & Research
Susan Beckett	Annie Dunaway	Beth Gilbert
Beth Kershner	Pat Lee	Janet Marsella
Katie O'Mary	Janice Perkins	Margaret Westberry

Computer	**Pre-Sales**	**Title**
Kathy Schmidt	Nancy Shelley	Karen Jackson

Publicity & Marketing
Pat Lee	Jeanne Seveska	Amy Short

Speakers Bureau	**Retail Sales**	**Tasting Coordination**
Chris Fox	Rosemary McKibben	Katie O'Mary

Distribution	**Consultant**
Patti Sanders	The Image Agency

Ex-Officio
Mary Kaye Bailey	Mitzi Chambers	Sharon Saliba	Jamie Shertzer

Without generous contributions of time, energy, expertise and resources from the following individuals and businesses, our *Sterling Service* would never have been published:

Mary Andrews	Melissa Bottger	Dothan Printing & Litho
Beryl Flowers	Carol Flowers	JoAnn Bell Gregory
Norma Hanson	Patsy Helms	William P. Hood, Jr., M.D.
Jackson Thornton & Co.	Robin Rainer	Ted's Jewelers

Our deepest gratitude goes to these **special contributors** and to anyone we may have inadvertently failed to mention!

Dothan Service League

Organized on May 22, 1946, the purpose of the Dothan Service League was and is to engage in work that we believe will enhance the quality of life of Dothan, Alabama residents.

During the past fifty years, the League has successfully undertaken, staffed and founded numerous projects, including the Red Cross, Dental Clinic, Boy Scouts, Girl Scouts, Motor Corp., Salvation Army, USO, Immunization Clinic, Community Chest (United Way), Family Life Conference, Gingerbread House Day Nursery, School Enrichment programs, Oral Polio Vaccine Drive, Maternity Clinic, Dothan Service League Girls' Club, Dyslexia Clinic, Meals on Wheels, Teacher's Aid programs, Senior Citizen programs at Evergreen Presbyterian Church, Southeast Alabama Medical Center Gift Shop, Child Abuse Program, Parents Anonymous (PACE), Project Noel, Children Can Soar program, Vaughn-Blumberg Center and "Miss Dothan" contest. The League also established the Town and Gown Theater, collected gifts for Partlow, sponsored candidates for Man and Woman of the Year and bagged two tons of peanuts for the National Peanut Festival. In addition to volunteer assistance by League members, these projects and organizations benefited from financial assistance in excess of $500,000 from the League.

Each year the League donates more than 6,000 volunteer hours and $36,000 to our community through organizations such as Children's Rehabilitation Services, Meals on Wheels, Evergreen Nutrition Program, Houston-Love Memorial Library, Southeast Alabama Medical Center Gift Shop, House of Ruth, Chrysalis, Wiregrass Hospice, Adolescent Resource Center, Girls Inc., ARC (Association for Retarded Citizens, Inc.), Alzheimer's Association and the Parent & Child Enrichment Center. We also maintain scholarships to Wallace College and Troy State University Dothan for local students.

In order to continue and expand our services to the Dothan community, we are publishing this cookbook in celebration of the past fifty years and in anticipation of the next fifty. All proceeds from the sale will become charitable contributions.

We, the members of the Dothan Service League, hope that our cookbook, a true labor of love, will encourage and enhance your *Sterling Service.*

Contributors

The Cookbook Committee of the Dothan Service League wishes to express sincere appreciation to the many contributors and testers, current and auxiliary members, without whose assistance during the last few years and support over the past fifty years, publication of this cookbook would not have been possible.

Mary Earle Adams
Mrs. William C. Adams
Glenda Price Albright
Mary S. Alford
Thresea F. Allen
Carol Andrews
Mrs. Max Andrews
Mrs. Paul Angeloff
June Austin
Mary Kaye Bailey
Mrs. W. F. Bailey
Mrs. Charles W. Baker
Mrs. Pete Barkley
Mrs. Troy Barrett
Mrs. Merrill Barron
Mrs. Ted Bauman
Mrs. Sid Beasley
Mrs. Edward Benak
Catherine H. Bennett
Mrs. Oliver Bentley
Brooksie S. Berry
Mrs. Bob Berryhill
Mrs. Jeff Bishop
Mrs. E. E. Bishop, Jr.
Mrs. E. E. Bishop, Sr.
Mrs. Charles Bloodworth
Mrs. William Blount
Mrs. Jeri Blumberg
Mrs. Richard Blumberg
Susan S. Blumberg
Mrs. Jack Blumenfeld
Nancy Bolin
Mrs. Alton Boyd
Mrs. Carl Brackin
Sue McNab Bradshaw
Mrs. Jay Bragg
Mrs. J. H. Brennan, Jr.
Mrs. William Brittain
Betty Ann Bronaugh
Robin Roseberry
  Brookshire

Mrs. Clarence Brown
Dani Marie H. Brown
Mrs. Merwyn Brown
Nancy N. Brown
Mrs. Clifton Lee Buck
Brenda Hall Burch
Mrs. Harold Burnham
Mrs. Michael Burnham
Mrs. E. G. Burson
Mrs. Ben Byrd
Mrs. Nagel Kirby Byrd
Mrs. Archie D.
  Carmichael, IV
Mrs. G. W. Carpenter
Mrs. Harry Carpenter
Mrs. Mac F. Carpenter
Paula G. Carson
Mrs. Andrew Carter
Mrs. Cada Carter
Mrs. Sam Casey, Jr.
Mitzi Murray Chambers
Mrs. Charles Chapman, Jr.
Mrs. Charles Chapman, III
Mrs. Leon Cheshire
Mrs. C. R. Church, Jr.
Mrs. Alan Clark
Mrs. Ken Clark
Mrs. Tal Clark
Mrs. Joel Clements
Mrs. Bob Coats
Sue Sessions Cobb
Mrs. Lawrence Coe
Mrs. Robert Coffman
Mrs. Jeff Coleman
Nona Colley
Mrs. Jack Cook
Mrs. Roddy Cook
Mrs. Robert Cooper
Mrs. Raymond Creel
Mrs. Herman Culpepper
Mrs. Richard Cundith

Connie Harper Darby
Mrs. Lan Darty
Mrs. David Dauphin
Mrs. James L. Davis
Mrs. Joanne Davis
Mrs. John C. Davis
Mrs. Pat Davis
Mrs. Rufus Davis
Mrs. Stafford Davis
Mrs. Donnie Dean
Mrs. Raymond F. Dees, Jr.
Kay M. DeLoney
Mrs. Roger Denisar
Mrs. Dan Denney
Mrs. Jack P. Dinkins
Mrs. Lee Dobbs
Mrs. Joseph Donofro
Mrs. Lex Dowling
Mrs. Mary Gene Dowling
Mrs. John Downs
Mrs. Ed Driggers
Mrs. Roy M. Driggers
Mrs. James B. Duke
Annie Paulk Dunaway
Mrs. Mark Dunning
Mrs. Mike Dunning
Diane H. Eaton
Pat Elliot
Mrs. Stanhope Elmore
Mrs. Rob Emblom
Mrs. Bob Embry
Becky Lane English
Mrs. Reece Ennis
Mrs. William L. Entz
Mrs. William G. Espy
Jim Ellis Etheridge
Mrs. Dave Eubank
Nancy D. Evans
Mrs. William M. Evans
Mrs. L. A. Farmer, Jr.
Mrs. Eugene Faulkner

Mrs. Paul Felts
Mrs. Alma Finney
Susan Fisher
Bonnie Flowers
Carol Morrow Flowers
Mrs. Drury Flowers
Mrs. F. A. Flowers, Jr.
Mrs. George Flowers
Mrs. John J. Flowers
Mrs. Paul Flowers, Jr.
Mary Lucy Campbell Floyd
Mrs. W. O. Floyd
Mrs. Gene Fogg
Mrs. Colon Folk
Mrs. John Forrester
Miriam B. Forrester
Mrs. Quay Fortner
Chris S. Fox
Mrs. E. B. Freeman
Mrs. Butch Frumin
Mrs. Frank M. Gaines
Mrs. Herbert Gannon
Mrs. Arthur Gardner
Mrs. Fred Garner
Mrs. Joe Garner
Mrs. Jo K. Garrett
Beth Burns Gilbert
Mrs. George Gilbert
Mrs. F. B. Gordy
Mrs. Wayne Granger
Mrs. James Grant
Mrs. Charles Grantland
Sue Mallory Green
Mrs. W. W. Gregory, Jr.
Mrs. Byron Griffin
Mrs. John D. Grigsby
Mrs. Louie D. Grimes
Mrs. W. B. Groover
Mrs. Clay Grubb
Mrs. Stephen Hale
Mrs. Ingraham Hanahan, Jr.
Mrs. Ingraham Hanahan, Sr.
Mrs. LaBruce Hanahan
Mrs. Donnie Hardy
Mrs. Charles Harmon
Judy Harris
Mrs. Bob Harris
Mrs. Daniel Harrison
Mrs. K. Lamar Hart
Mrs. Mark Hartzog
Mrs. Mary Hartzog

Mrs. B. E. Hathcock
Mrs. Davis Haughton
Carolyn B. Hawkins
Mrs. R. Paul Hayes
Mrs. Dan D. Helms
Mrs. William Henderson
Mrs. Margaret Hendricks
Mrs. Robert S. Hewes
Mrs. Charles Heyman
Mrs. Roby Hicks
Mrs. Warren Hilson
Grace Collins Hodges
Mrs. Jack Holland
Mrs. James Holland
Cindy Solomon Hollis
Mrs. Janice W. Hollis
Mrs. Hugh Holloway
Mrs. Robert Holmes
Mrs. Tony Holmes
Mrs. Clay Howell
Mrs. Harry C. Howell
Mary Howell
Mrs. Mike Howell
Mrs. Barnett C. Hudson
Mrs. Ann Hundley
Mrs. Randy Hurst
Mrs. Dow Husky
Evelyn Mullen Isbell
Mrs. David Jackson
Mrs. Raymond Jackson
Mrs. Jane Johnson
Mrs. Louis Johnson
Mrs. Olen D. Johnson
Pat B. Johnson
Sara Gene Johnston
Clare A. Jones
Florrie Jones
Mrs. Gary Jones
Mrs. James M. Jones, Jr.
Lyndall Major Jones
Mrs. Patrick Jones
Mrs. Steve Jordan
Mrs. Lamar Judah
Mrs. Jack W. Kale, Jr.
Ruthann Kamstra
Linda S. Kelly
Sheila Overton Kelly
Mrs. Don Kennington
Mrs. Mark Kershner
Lea Kelley King
Mrs. Thomas M. Kirkland

Mrs. Larry Knight
Mrs. Andrew J. Kosan
Mrs. Jim Lambert
Mrs. Kathryn Lane
Pat Henry Lee
Rosa Lee
Mrs. William L. Lee
Mrs. Milton Lennicx
Mrs. Don Lewis
Mrs. Roys Lewis
Mrs. George Lindholm
Mrs. Raymond Lindsey
Mrs. Alan Livingston
Mrs. Walter Long
Mrs. William J. Lupinacci
Mrs. Douglas Lurie
Mary Geiger Maddox
Mrs. Davis Malone
Rulene L. Manuel
Roberta Greenberg
   Marblestone
Karen W. Marcilliat
Mrs. Ralph Marcus
Mrs. Martin Margolies
Mrs. Sam Marley
Sherry J. Marlow
Mrs. Jerry Marsella
Mrs. James F. Martin
Lisa M. Martin
Mrs. Mike Martin
Vicki Maddox Martin
Denise R. Mashburn
Mrs. Rafael Mayor
Mrs. Bill McCamy
Mrs. Steve McCarroll
Mrs. Robert McCarty
Mrs. Richmond McClintock
Mrs. Gary McCord
Mrs. John McCullough
Mrs. E. B. McDaniel, Jr.
Mrs. William McFatter
Mrs. James McGouirk
Lisa Wood McGowan
Mrs. Gene McGriff
Mrs. Dwight McInish
Rosemary Grant McKibben
Mrs. John McLean
Mrs. Don McMullan
Mrs. J. H. McMullan
Mrs. Brady E. Mendheim
Mrs. Phillip Merrill

Audrey McKissick Miller
Marge Ann Minkiewicz
Mrs. Faith Miskell
Mrs. Earle C. Moody
Mrs. Cyndie Moore
Jennifer Cummings Moore
Mrs. Robert Moore
Mrs. Richard Morgan
Mrs. Dan Morris
Mrs. Bill Mullen
Mrs. Charles Nailen
Mrs. Charles Nesbitt
Mrs. Rhonda Nichols
Ruth Nomberg
Mrs. William Nomberg
Beth Ross Nowell
Mrs. Tate O'Brian
Mrs. Joseph O'Byrne
Katie Mears O'Mary
Mrs. James C. Owen
Mrs. Howard J. Owens
Mrs. J. W. Parkman, Jr.
Mrs. Harrison Parrish
Mrs. Tyrone Parrish
Mrs. W. T. Parrish
Mrs. Jane Payne
Donna Weatherly Pearce
Debra Perkins
Janice N. Perkins
Mrs. Gerald Penn
Mrs. Larry Pike
Michelle Miller Plagenhoef
Mrs. Coy Poitevint
Mrs. Dennis Powell
Susan G. Price
Mrs. Wilton Pruitt
Mrs. Jane Ramsey
Mrs. Joel Ramsey
Mrs. Larry Register
Mrs. David Ritchie
Mrs. Carl Roberts
Mrs. Jabus Roberts
Mrs. James Robertson
Linda Robertson
Anita W. Robinson
Mrs. James L. Rodgers
Kay Finney Roney
Pat Ross
Mrs. George Saad
Mrs. Mark Saliba

Mrs. June Sanders
Patti Bryant Sanders
Mrs. James Sawyer
Mrs. David Scarborough
Mrs. T. R. Scheile
Kathy Schmidt
Janice Schwadron
Mrs. Ron Sealock
Becky Mallory Searcy
Mrs. Ralph Segrest
Beth Sanderson Shealy
Mrs. William P. Shealy
Joan T. Sheffield
Nancy Logan Shelley
Mrs. Neil Shelor
Mrs. Jamie Shertzer
Amy Dove Short
Mrs. M. E. Sigmon
Mrs. Agnes Simpson
Mrs. Jack Sitkin
Sharon Tew Sizemore
Mrs. Charles E. Skeen
Mrs. James M. Smith
Mrs. Jerry D. Smith
Karen Smith
Mrs. O. Darrell Smith
Mrs. Rufus Smith
Mrs. Arch Solomon
Mrs. Art Solomon
Mrs. N. B. Solomon
Mrs. Phillip Spann
Mrs. William C. Spires
Mrs. Henry Sprouse
Mrs. M. J. Steensland
Angelia Stokes
Mrs. Harmon Stokes
Mrs. Sandra Stokes
Mrs. James Stuckey, Jr.
Mrs. Wilton Sturges, Jr.
Mrs. James Sullivan
Mrs. Charles G. Taylor
Janet J. Taylor
Mrs. Bo Thagard
Mrs. Bob Theune
Mikell E. Thomas
Mrs. Martha Thomley
Mrs. William Thompson
Mrs. James T. Thrower
Mrs. James L. Tindell
Mrs. R. L. Tindell

Mrs. Sam Torrence
Mrs. Watson Turk
Mrs. Sib Turner
Mona Gallion Ullmann
Mrs. Jerome Varnum
Mrs. Henry Vaughn, Jr.
Mrs. George Veale
Mrs. William N. Veale
Mrs. Ruud Veltman
Mrs. Rodney Vickery
Mrs. Otto Voelinger, Jr.
Mrs. Otto Voelinger
Mrs. Alan Wages
Mrs. David Walden
Mrs. Joe Walden
Mrs. J. Ken Wallace
Mrs. J. A. Ward, Jr.
Kathy Bryant Ware
Margaret Lee Watson
Mrs. William Watson
Mrs. Garrison Watts
Mrs. William T. Weissinger
Mrs. Allen Wells
Mrs. T. Wayne Wells
Mrs. Theron Wells
Margaret Carolyn
  Westberry
Mrs. Sam Wexler
Mrs. Ansley Whatley, Jr.
Mrs. Charles Whiddon
Mrs. Howard Whitaker
Mrs. Edwin Whitehead
Mrs. Herb Whitestone
Mrs. Gwen Williams
Mrs. Mykle Williams
Mrs. Sam Williams, Jr.
Mrs. Ted Williams
Mrs. W. D. Williams
Anne Wilson
Mrs. George Wilson
Mrs. John Wilson
Mrs. S. W. Windham
Mrs. Glen F. Wise
Mrs. Robert Woodall
Jean P. Woodham
Mrs. Henry W. Wright
Mrs. David Wuertzer
Mrs. David M. Wynne

Table of Contents

Measurements and Equivalents

pinch or dash . . . . less than ⅛ t.

60 drops . . . . 1 t.
3 t. . . . . 1 T.

2 T. . . . . 1 fl. oz.
1 jigger . . . . 1½ fl. oz.

½ c. . . . . 8 T.
½ c. . . . . 4 fl. oz.

⅝ c. . . . . ½ c. + 2 T.
⅝ c. . . . . 10 T.

⅓ c. . . . . 5 T. + 1 t.
⅔ c. . . . . 10 T. + 2 t.
⅔ c. . . . . 5⅓ fl. oz.

¾ c. . . . . 12 T.
¾ c. . . . . 6 fl. oz.

⅞ c. . . . . ¾ c. + 2 T.
⅞ c. . . . . 14 T.

1 c. . . . . 16 T.
1 c. . . . . 8 fl. oz.
1 c. . . . . ½ pt.

1¼ c. . . . . 10 fl. oz.
1⅓ c. . . . . 10⅔ fl. oz.
1½ c. . . . . 12 fl. oz.
1⅔ c. . . . . 13⅓ fl. oz.
1¾ c. . . . . 14 fl. oz.

2 c. . . . . 16 fl. oz.
2 c. . . . . 1 pt.

2½ c. . . . . 20 fl. oz.

3 c. . . . . 24 fl. oz.
3 c. . . . . ¾ qt.

3½ c. . . . . 28 fl. oz.
3½ c. . . . . ⅞ qt.

4 c. . . . . 1 qt.

1/16 pt. . . . . 2 T.
⅛ pt. . . . . ¼ c.
¼ pt. . . . . ½ c.
⅓ pt. . . . . ⅔ c.
⅜ pt. . . . . ¾ c.
½ pt. . . . . 1 c.
⅔ pt. . . . . 1⅓ c.
⅝ pt. . . . . 1¼ c.
¾ pt. . . . . 1½ c.
⅞ pt. . . . . 1¾ c.

1 pt. . . . . 2 c.

1/16 qt. . . . . ¼ c.
⅛ qt. . . . . ½ c.
¼ qt. . . . . 1 c.
⅓ qt. . . . . 1⅓ c.
⅜ qt. . . . . 1½ c.
½ qt. . . . . 2 c.
⅝ qt. . . . . 2½ c.
¾ qt. . . . . 3 c.
⅞ qt. . . . . 3½ c.

1 qt. . . . . 4 c.
1 qt. . . . . 2 pt.
1 qt. . . . . ¼ gal.
1 qt. . . . . 32 fl. oz.
1 qt. . . . . .946 liters

1 liter . . . . 1.06 qt.
1 liter . . . . 4 c. + 3⅓ T.

5 c. . . . . 40 fl. oz.

6 c. . . . . 1½ qt.
6 c. . . . . 48 fl. oz.

10 c. . . . . 2½ qt.
10 c. . . . . 80 fl. oz.

12 c. . . . . 3 qt.
12 c. . . . . 96 fl. oz.

3 qt.	12 c.
3 qt.	¾ gal.
4 qt.	1 gal.
4 qt.	128 fl. oz.
¹⁄₁₆ gal.	¼ c.
⅛ gal.	½ qt.
¼ gal.	1 qt.
⅓ gal.	1⅓ qt.
⅜ gal.	1½ qt.
½ gal.	2 qt.
⅝ gal.	2½ qt.
⅔ gal.	2⅔ qt.
¾ gal.	3 qt.
⅞ gal.	3½ qt.
1 gal.	4 qt.
1 gal.	8 pt.
1 gal.	16 c.

Dry Weights

2 gal.	1 peck
8 qt.	1 peck
1 peck	8 qt.
1 peck	2 gal.
4 pecks	1 bushel
1 bushel	4 pecks
1 bushel	8 gal.
1 bushel	32 qt.
1 bushel	64 pt.
1 bushel	128 c.
¼ lb.	4 oz.
½ lb.	8 oz.
1 lb.	16 oz.
2.2 lb.	1 kilo

Total Volume of Common Baking Pans

Ring Molds	8½ x 2¼ in. mold	4½ c.
	9¼ x 2¾ in. mold	8 c.
Spring Form Pans	8 x 3 in. pan	12 c.
	9 x 3 in. pan	16 c.
Pie Plates	9 in. plate	4 c.
	10 in. plate	6 c.
Cake Pans	8 x 1¼ in. layer pan	4 c.
	8 or 9 in. layer pan	6 c.
Loaf Pans	7⅜ x 3⅝ x 2¼ in. pan	4 c.
	8½ x 3⅝ x 2⅝ in. pan	6 c.
	9 x 5 x 3 in. pan	8 c.
Square Pans	8 x 8 x 2 in. pan	8 c.
	9 x 9 x 2 in. pan	10 c.
Baking Pans and Dishes	11 x 7 x 1½ in. dish	8 c.
	11¾ x 7½ x 1¾ in. pan	10 c.
	13½ x 8½ x 2 in. glass dish	12 c.
	13 x 9 x 2 in. metal pan	15 c.
Jelly-Roll Pan	15 x 10 x 1 in. pan	10 c.

Entertaining in the Twenty-First Century

Since 9-11, volunteerism and returning to our family and home values have caused cookbook sales to go through the roof. Many of us have returned to the kitchen to provide the love and safety that we knew as children through our mom's cooking. With that in mind we are reprinting our tribute to that era, *Sterling Service*. This era of home cooked meals with our family gathered around the big table, using our sterling pieces and good china, makes us feel safe and secure. It provides us with the ability to continue amongst the trials and tribulations of life. Food provides us with comfort to both our stomachs and our souls. Dothan Service League provides comfort to many in the community. We have been able to provide through the profits from this cookbook for many meals (Meals on Wheels / Dorothy Quick Nutrition Center) and other comforts through helping at Children's Rehab, donations to House of Ruth, the Salvation Army and many other worthy organizations in the Wiregrass Area. Our cookbook title is appropriate for all we do, our Service to the community has been quite Sterling.

We would like to recognize one of our own, Elizabeth Crockett, Alabama's Junior Miss and congratulate her on her accomplish-ments. She is one of ours because we can count many of her relatives as members. Elizabeth's mother, Olivia, was instrumental in keeping the cookbook going. Her grandmother, great-aunt and aunt have all been in Service League and have served the community well. Elizabeth won a $2,500 "Best Recipe" Award from Tyson Foods during the 2003 American's Junior Miss. We wanted to make sure that everyone could enjoy her award so we are including her recipe, Purse de Poulet, on page 89 in this reprint. Congrats, Elizabeth.

Thanks for allowing us the privilege of being the Cookbook Chairmen during this exciting time. We have loved every minute of it!

Pamela Pitman Brown   2002-2003 Chairman
Juanita Sykes   2003-2004 Chairman

Prelude

Appetizers and Beverages

Prelude
Appetizers and Beverages

Prelude

International Silver Company
Meriden, Connecticut

Prelude was introduced in 1939, near the end of the Art Deco era. Embellished with a small cluster of flowers at its base, the slender-necked stem expands gracefully into a fluted terminal which is undecorated except for a cap of flowers and foliage at the tip. Designed by Alfred J. Kintz, who created many patterns over a career with International that spanned 45 years, Prelude has been a consistent favorite since it was first made.

The International Silver Company was formed in 1898 by the amalgamation of a number of smaller companies and eventually became the largest manufacturer of silverware in the world. Among the illustrious companies which originally or later became part of International were Webster & Son; Derby Silver Company; Simpson, Hall and Miller; Meriden Brittania Company; Rogers Brothers and many others. In 1984, International was bought by Katy Industries, Inc., Elgin, Illinois, which was already the owner of Wallace Silversmiths. The company is now known as Wallace International Silversmiths.

Pictured: Kenmare crystal by Waterford, Melrose
cocktail forks and Prelude place setting

Pesto Pasta Rolls

6 lasagna noodles	¼ cup pesto sauce
4 ounces softened cream cheese	2 (2½-ounce) packages of thinly sliced ham or pastrami
1 tablespoon water	green leaf lettuce
¼ cup sliced black olives	
¼ cup chopped, sweet red pepper	

- Cook lasagna noodles according to package directions. Pat dry and cover with moist paper towel to keep from drying out.
- Stir water into cream cheese to thin. Blend black olives and red pepper into cream cheese and spread cream cheese mixture on one side of each noodle.
- Spread pesto on top of cream cheese mixture.
- Top pesto with a lettuce leaf.
- Divide the meat among noodles.
- Roll up noodles tightly, jelly-roll-style.
- Place rolls, seam side down, on a platter lined with lettuce. If necessary, secure with toothpicks.
- Cover and chill 2 hours or until ready to serve.
- To serve, cut each roll into thin slices.

Serves 24

Crabmeat and Avocado Appetizers

1 (6-ounce) package frozen snow crabmeat	2 tablespoons mayonnaise
12 slices white bread	1 teaspoon lemon juice
1 avocado	¼ teaspoon onion powder
4 ounces cream cheese	2 drops red pepper sauce

- Thaw and drain crabmeat.
- Trim crusts from bread. Cut each slice into triangles.
- Toast bread under broiler on one side.
- In blender or food processor, combine avocado, cream cheese, mayonnaise, lemon juice, onion powder and pepper sauce.
- Spread toast triangles with avocado mixture and top with crabmeat.

Serves 24

Salmon-Stuffed Snow Peas

1 (8-ounce) package softened cream cheese

2 tablespoons fresh lemon juice

1 (3-ounce) can pink salmon, cleaned and drained

2 boxes frozen snow peas

- Combine cream cheese and lemon juice.
- Add salmon.
- Blanche snow peas 1 minute.
- Rinse with cold water to set.
- Cool.
- String and gently split open peas.
- Using cookie press or pastry bag, stuff peas with salmon mixture.
- Keep refrigerated until ready to serve.

Serves 20

Mustard Shrimp and Tortellini

¼ cup tarragon vinegar

¼ cup red wine vinegar

1 teaspoon black pepper

¼ cup dry mustard

1 teaspoon hot pepper flakes

2 teaspoons salt

¼ cup vegetable oil

¼ cup olive oil

¼ cup chopped parsley

2 cloves minced garlic

6 chopped scallions

¼ cup capers, drained

2½ pounds cooked, medium shrimp

1 pound cheese tortellini, cooked and cooled (2 cups)

- Mix together tarragon and red wine vinegars, black pepper, mustard, hot pepper flakes, salt, oils, parsley, garlic, scallions and capers. Set aside.
- In large dish mix shrimp and cheese tortellini.
- Pour marinade over shrimp and tortellini.
- Refrigerate for 8 hours. Serve cold.

Serves 8-10

Pickled Shrimp

2½ pounds shrimp
    (fresh or frozen)
½ cup celery tops
¼ cup mixed pickling spices
    or ¼ cup shrimp boil
5 teaspoons salt, divided
2 cups sliced onions

7 bay leaves
1¼ cups salad oil
¾ cup white vinegar
2½ teaspoons capers
1½-2½ teaspoons celery seed
    dash of red pepper sauce

- Cover shrimp, in shell, in boiling water.
- Add celery tops, pickling spices and 3½ teaspoons salt.
- Cover and simmer 5 minutes.
- Drain and cool under water.
- Peel shells from shrimp and devein.
- Alternate cleaned shrimp and onions in shallow dish.
- Add bay leaves.
- Combine salad oil, white vinegar, capers, celery seed, 1½ teaspoons salt and red pepper sauce.
- Pour over shrimp.
- Cover and marinate at least 24 hours in the refrigerator.

Serves 10-15

Shrimp Dip

1 (8-ounce) package softened
    cream cheese
1 cup mayonnaise
2 (4¼-ounce) cans shrimp,
    drained and mashed
1 (6½-ounce) can minced
    clams, undrained

½ cup minced onions
1 cup finely chopped celery
1 teaspoon lemon juice
    salt and pepper to taste
    crackers or chips

- Mix cream cheese and mayonnaise together.
- Add shrimp, clams, onion, celery, lemon juice, salt and pepper.
- Chill.
- Serve with crackers or chips.

Yields 1½ cups

Cheese Pâté

1 (8-ounce) package softened
   cream cheese
1 cup shredded, sharp
   Cheddar cheese
4 teaspoons dry sherry
½ teaspoon curry powder

¼ teaspoon salt
1 (8-ounce) jar chopped
   chutney
3-4 chopped scallions
   (including tops)
   sesame or wheat crackers

- Combine cream cheese, cheddar cheese, sherry, curry powder and salt; mix thoroughly.
- Spread ½-inch thick on serving platter.
- Chill until firm.
- Spread chutney over top.
- Sprinkle with scallions.
- Serve with crackers.

Serves 8

Crabmeat Pâté

2 tablespoons chili sauce
½ cup chopped celery
1 cup chopped scallions
1 teaspoon chopped parsley

½ teaspoon hot pepper sauce
½ cup mayonnaise
1 pound lump crabmeat
   assorted crackers

- Mix chili sauce, celery, scallions, parsley, hot pepper sauce and mayonnaise.
- Gently stir in crabmeat.
- Form into a ball.
- Serve with crackers.

Serves 10-12

Caviar Supreme

1 envelope unflavored gelatin	dash of red pepper sauce
¼ cup cold water	1 puréed medium avocado
4 chopped, hard-cooked eggs	1 diced medium avocado
½ cup + 2 tablespoons mayonnaise, divided	2 tablespoons fresh lemon juice
2 chopped shallots, divided freshly ground, white pepper	1 (8-ounce) carton sour cream
¼ cup chopped parsley	1 (4-ounce) jar red or black caviar
1¼ teaspoons salt, divided	dark pumpernickel bread

- Dissolve gelatin in cold water. Microwave on high 20 seconds to liquefy. Set aside.
- Mix chopped eggs, ½ cup mayonnaise, ½ of a chopped shallot, dash of white pepper, parsley, ¾ teaspoon salt and dash of red pepper sauce.
- Add 1 tablespoon of gelatin mixture.
- Spread on bottom of well greased 9-inch spring-form pan.
- Refrigerate while mixing next layer.
- Blend both avocados, 1 chopped shallot, 2 tablespoons mayonnaise, dash of red pepper sauce, lemon juice, ½ teaspoon salt, dash of white pepper and 1 tablespoon of gelatin mixture.
- Spread evenly over base layer.
- Refrigerate.
- Mix sour cream, ½ of a chopped shallot and remainder of gelatin.
- Spread carefully over second layer.
- Cover tightly with plastic wrap.
- Chill thoroughly (8 hours or overnight).
- Remove side of pan to serve.
- Rinse and drain caviar very well. Sprinkle on top.
- Serve with finger slices of pumpernickel bread.
- Use within 24 hours of preparation.

Serves 25

Pesto Cheese Torte

8	cloves minced garlic, divided	½	teaspoon salt
2	cups fresh basil leaves	½	teaspoon black pepper
1	cup virgin olive oil	1	cup walnuts or pine nuts
1	cup grated Parmesan cheese	4	(8-ounce) packages softened cream cheese
¼	cup Romano cheese	2	tablespoons lemon juice
			assorted crackers

- To make pesto, place 4 cloves minced garlic and basil in food processor.
- With motor running, drizzle in oil.
- Add Parmesan and Romano cheeses, salt, pepper and nuts.
- Pulse to blend.
- In a separate container, beat cream cheese, lemon juice and remaining ½ of minced garlic until smooth.
- Cut 2 18-inch squares of cheesecloth. Lightly moisten and use to line 5- to 6-cup mold.
- Place ½ of cheese mixture in mold.
- Add pesto.
- Cover with remaining cheese.
- Fold cloth ends over cheese and lightly compress.
- Chill 2 hours.
- Invert onto serving dish and remove cheesecloth.
- Garnish with fresh basil.
- Serve with crackers.

Serves 25

Cucumber-Shrimp Crescents

½	cup finely chopped cucumber	1	tablespoon French salad dressing
1	teaspoon chopped chives	1	tablespoon mayonnaise
½	pound chopped, cooked shrimp		white bread

- Combine cucumber, chives, shrimp, salad dressing and mayonnaise.
- Cut white bread into crescent shapes.
- Spread mixture onto bread slices.

Yields 12 crescents

Beer and Cheese Spread

2	cups shredded, sharp Cheddar cheese	½	teaspoon dry mustard
2	cups shredded Swiss cheese	1	clove minced garlic
1	teaspoon Worcestershire sauce	½-⅓	cup beer
			assorted crackers or rye bread rounds

- Have Cheddar and Swiss cheeses at room temperature.
- In food processor, grate cheeses together.
- Add Worcestershire sauce, mustard and garlic.
- Beat in enough beer to make cheese spread smoothly.
- Serve at room temperature with crackers or rye bread rounds.

Yields 2 cups

Avocado Dip

1	finely chopped, ripened avocado	1	(4¼-ounce) can sliced, ripe olives, drained
1	peeled and chopped tomato	6	tablespoons Italian salad dressing
5	chopped scallions		salt and pepper to taste
1	(4¼-ounce) can chopped green chilies, drained		corn chips

- Mix avocado, tomato, scallions, green chilies, olives and salad dressing.
- Add salt and pepper. Let season several hours in refrigerator before serving.
- Goes well with corn chips.

Serves 6-8

Fiesta Cheesecake

1½ cups finely crushed tortilla
  chips
¼ cup melted butter
¼ cup grated Monterey Jack
  cheese
2 (8-ounce) packages
  softened cream cheese
2 eggs
1 (10-ounce) package grated
  Monterey Jack cheese
1 (4-ounce) can chopped
  green chilies, drained

¼ teaspoon ground red
  pepper
1 (8-ounce) carton sour
  cream
½ cup chopped green pepper
½ cup chopped yellow
  pepper
½ cup chopped red pepper
½ cup chopped scallions
1 medium diced tomato
  chopped black olives and
  cilantro for garnish
  tortilla chips

- Preheat oven to 325 degrees.
- Mix crushed tortilla chips, butter and ¼ cup Monterey Jack cheese.
- Place in lightly greased 9-inch spring-form pan. Press evenly on bottom of pan.
- Bake 15 minutes.
- Remove from oven and cool.
- Beat cream cheese until smooth. Add eggs.
- Stir in 10 ounces of Monterey Jack cheese, chilies and red pepper.
- Pour over crust in spring-form pan.
- Bake 30 minutes.
- Cool 10 minutes.
- Run knife around edge of pan to loosen cheesecake. Remove side of pan.
- Cool completely.
- Spread sour cream on top.
- Cover and chill.
- Garnish with remaining peppers, scallions, tomato, olives and cilantro before serving.
- Serve with tortilla chips.

Serves 25

Ensenada Salsa

2   chopped medium tomatoes
1   bunch chopped scallions
1   (4½-ounce) can jalapeño
     peppers
1   (4½-ounce) can chopped,
     ripe olives

3   tablespoons olive oil
1½ tablespoons white wine
     vinegar
2   teaspoons garlic salt
     tortilla chips

- Combine tomatoes, scallions, jalapeño peppers, olives, olive oil, white wine vinegar and garlic salt.
- Refrigerate.
- Serve with tortilla chips.

Yields 2 cups

Mexican Pinwheels

1   (8-ounce) carton sour
     cream
1   (8-ounce) package softened
     cream cheese
1   (4-ounce) can chopped
     black olives

1   (4-ounce) jar chopped
     green olives
½   cup chopped scallions
2   finely chopped jalapeños
1   cup shredded Cheddar
     cheese
5   (10-inch) flour tortillas

- Mix sour cream and cream cheese.
- Add black and green olives, scallions, jalapeños and Cheddar cheese and mix well.
- Spread on tortilla. Roll tortilla up jelly-roll-style.
- Wrap in plastic wrap.
- Chill overnight.
- Slice the following day.

Serves 8-10

Mock Smoked Salmon

1	can salmon	2	tablespoons grated onion
1	(8-ounce) package softened cream cheese	¼	teaspoon salt
		¼	teaspoon liquid smoke
2	tablespoons red horseradish	¾	cup crushed pecans, divided
1	tablespoon lemon juice	¼	cup minced parsley
1	tablespoon Worcestershire sauce		

- Drain and bone salmon.
- Combine cream cheese, horseradish, lemon juice, Worcestershire sauce, onion, salt, liquid smoke and ½ cup pecans. Mix well and form ball.
- Chill 2 hours.
- Shape into log.
- Roll log in remaining ¼ cup pecans and parsley.

Serves 15-20

Chicken-Curry Balls

1	cup toasted almonds	1	tablespoon chutney
4	ounces softened cream cheese	½-¾	teaspoon salt
2	tablespoons mayonnaise	⅛	teaspoon cayenne pepper (optional)
1	cup chopped, cooked chicken	½	cup fresh or frozen coconut
1	tablespoon curry powder		

- Chop toasted almonds or put through food processor.
- Mix cream cheese, mayonnaise, chicken, curry, chutney and salt. Add cayenne pepper if desired.
- Roll mixture into walnut-size balls.
- Roll balls in coconut.
- Chill.
- Display in hollowed, fresh coconut. Fill coconut with balls and allow some to cascade over the sides.
- Accent with fresh apricots and tropical flowers.

Yields 2 dozen balls

Spicy Beef Bites

1 (3-ounce) package softened cream cheese
¼ cup grated onion

1-2 tablespoons milk
¼ pound spiced beef

- Mix onion into cream cheese.
- Add 1-2 tablespoons of milk, so it will spread easily.
- Smooth out one slice of beef.
- Spread cheese mixture onto beef slice.
- Top with another slice of beef.
- Roll up jelly-roll-style and fasten with a toothpick.
- Chill.
- Cut each roll into 4-5 bite-size pieces.
- Stick a colored toothpick in each piece.

Yields 18 roll-ups

Proscuitto Olive Cheese Ball

1 (3-ounce) package softened cream cheese
1 (8-ounce) package softened cream cheese
½ cup thinly sliced proscuitto
2 cups shredded Cheddar cheese
2 tablespoons finely chopped olives

1 tablespoon prepared mustard
¼ teaspoon dry mustard
¼ teaspoon red pepper
¾ teaspoon chopped chives
¼ teaspoon celery seed
⅛ teaspoon salt
1 clove minced garlic
½ cup chopped pecans
assorted crackers

- Combine cream cheese, proscuitto, Cheddar cheese, olives, mustards, red pepper, chives, celery seed, salt and garlic and mix well.
- Shape mixture into a ball and roll in pecans.
- Chill well.
- Serve with assorted crackers.
- Make cheese ball several days in advance for full flavor. It freezes well.

Yields 2 cups

White Cheddar Cheese Ball with Raspberry Preserves

1 (10-ounce) package Vermont white Cheddar	2 tablespoons mayonnaise
2 tablespoons diced onion	½ cup raspberry jam
	assorted crackers

- Process Cheddar, onion and mayonnaise in a food processor. If processor is not available, grate cheese and mix in onions and mayonnaise with hands.
- Form into a ball.
- Pour raspberry jam over cheese ball.
- Serve with crackers.

Yields 2 cups

Pecan-Glazed Brie

1 cup packed brown sugar	1 (8-inch) wheel of Brie cheese, top rind cut off, at room temperature
⅓ cup water	
¼ cup half-and-half	
¼ cup unsalted butter	apple wedges, crackers or fresh baked bread
¾ cup sweet and spicy pecans	

- Combine brown sugar and water in saucepan and bring to a boil.
- Cook over medium heat until mixture reaches the soft-ball stage, about 4 minutes from the time the mixture begins to boil.
- Cool the mixture slightly.
- Slowly stir in the half-and-half.
- Boil for another 3 or 4 minutes until the mixture is glossy and slightly thickened.
- Remove from heat and stir in the butter.
- Fold in sweet and spicy pecans.
- Pour the sweet and spicy glaze evenly over the top of cheese so it coats the top surface and runs a little over the side.
- Serve with apple wedges, crackers or fresh baked bread.

Serves 15

Sweet and Spicy Pecans

1	cup unsalted butter	1	tablespoon ground cumin
3	cups packed brown sugar	1	egg white
2	teaspoons dry mustard	1	pound shelled pecan
1	teaspoon cayenne pepper		halves

- Preheat oven to 300 degrees.
- Melt butter in large skillet.
- Add brown sugar, mustard, cayenne pepper and cumin.
- Remove from heat and stir to dissolve.
- Let cool, then stir in egg white.
- Pour mixture over pecans in a large bowl.
- Stir and toss until pecans are evenly coated.
- Spread coated pecans on baking sheet in a single layer.
- Bake for 20 minutes, shaking and tossing 2-3 times during cooking until golden brown.
- Once pecans are cool enough to handle, rub pecans between your hands to evenly distribute sugar coating and avoid clumping.
- Cool completely.

Yields 1 pound

Bacon and Tomato Cocktail Rounds

1	cup mayonnaise	36	thin slices fresh, white
1	tablespoon minced garlic		bread
2	tablespoons finely chopped	½	pound chopped, cooked
	onion		bacon
1	teaspoon salt	¼	cup finely chopped
12	plum or Italian tomatoes		scallions

- Combine mayonnaise, garlic, onion and salt. Chill.
- Cut off top of tomatoes. Slice lengthwise into thin slices.
- Cut bread into rounds with biscuit cutter or glass.
- Spread bread with mayonnaise mixture. Top with tomato slice and sprinkle with bacon then scallions.

Yields 36 rounds

Asparagus Roll-Ups

½ cup butter
1 tablespoon minced onion
1 tablespoon lemon juice
1 (3-ounce) package cream
  cheese
2 slices cooked, crumbled
  bacon

1 tablespoon Parmesan
  cheese
24 slices white bread
1 can asparagus spears,
  drained
¼ cup melted butter
  sliced black olives
  pimento slices

- Preheat oven to 350 degrees.
- Mix butter, onion, lemon juice, cream cheese, bacon and Parmesan cheese; set aside.
- Trim crust from bread and press each slice to ⅛-inch thickness with fingertips or rolling pin.
- Spread each slice with a slightly rounded teaspoonful of butter mixture.
- Place an asparagus spear on each slice with tip extending over one edge.
- Roll up tightly; secure with a wooden pick.
- Brush rolls with melted butter and place on ungreased baking sheet.
- Bake for 30 minutes.
- Remove picks and serve warm.
- Garnish with black olive slices and pimento.
- To freeze, do not brush with melted butter. Place unbaked rolls in an airtight container in freezer. To serve, remove from freezer, brush with melted butter and bake at 350 degrees for 30 minutes.

Yields 24 roll-ups

Clever Ways to Use Kitchen Scissors

Buy inexpensive scissors at the fabric store or discount store and:
- Snip bunches of chives or scallions.
- Cube chicken breast meat. First cut breast into strips, then cross cut (faster than a knife).
- Chop parsley or rosemary leaves. Put cleaned, stripped leaves in a juice glass or glass measuring cup. Stick scissors into vessel and cut until herb is chopped fine enough.
- Cut cooked bacon strips.

Artichoke Squares

1	(6-ounce) jar marinated artichoke hearts	¼	cup fine bread crumbs
1	(14-ounce) can plain artichoke hearts	¼	teaspoon salt
1	small finely chopped onion	⅛	teaspoon oregano
1	clove minced garlic	¼	teaspoon hot pepper sauce
4	eggs	½	pound shredded sharp Cheddar cheese
		2	teaspoons minced parsley

- Preheat oven to 325 degrees.
- Drain marinade from jar of artichokes into skillet.
- Drain juice from can of plain artichokes and discard juice.
- Chop all artichokes into small pieces and set aside.
- Add onion and garlic to skillet and sauté until clear.
- Beat eggs, and add bread crumbs, salt, oregano and hot pepper sauce.
- Stir in cheese, parsley, artichokes and onion mixture.
- Turn into a greased 10x6-inch baking pan.
- Bake for 30 minutes.
- Allow to cool in pan.
- Cut into 1-inch squares.
- Serve hot or cold. Freezes well.

Yields 60 squares

Pepperoni Mini-Muffins

1	cup all-purpose flour	1	egg
¼	cup grated Parmesan or Romano cheese	1	teaspoon baking powder
1	cup milk	½	stick diced pepperoni

- Preheat oven to 350 degrees.
- Combine flour, cheese, milk, egg, baking powder and pepperoni in a large bowl and mix well.
- Spoon into well greased mini muffin tins, filling to top of each muffin cup.
- Bake for 20 minutes, until brown.

Yields 24 mini-muffins

Mushroom Caps

18 large mushrooms	½ cup freshly grated
¼ cup butter	Parmesan cheese
6 minced scallions	red pepper or tomato for
1 package frozen spinach	garnish
soufflé, thawed	

- Remove and discard stems from mushrooms.
- Sauté mushroom caps in butter.
- Remove mushrooms and place them to drain.
- Sauté scallions in butter until soft.
- Add spinach soufflé and mix well.
- Place mixture in each cap.
- Sprinkle with Parmesan cheese and heat under broiler.
- Garnish with slices of red pepper or edge of tomato.

Serves 6-8

Crab-Filled Mushrooms

24 large mushrooms	2 tablespoons chopped red
6 ounces frozen crabmeat,	pepper
thawed	½ tablespoon dry sherry
¼ cup fine bread crumbs	1 teaspoon Dijon mustard
¼ cup sour cream	several dashes of hot
2 tablespoons melted butter	pepper sauce

- Remove and discard stems from mushrooms.
- Steam mushroom caps 3 minutes in steamer.
- Drain mushrooms.
- Drain and chop crabmeat.
- Mix crabmeat, bread crumbs, sour cream, butter, red pepper, sherry, mustard and hot pepper sauce in bowl and mix well.
- Stuff each mushroom cap with mixture.
- Place in 9x13-inch baking dish.
- Chill covered for several hours.
- Preheat oven to 425 degrees.
- Bake for 8-10 minutes.

Serves 12

Mushroom Pinwheels

2 packages refrigerated crescent rolls

1 (8-ounce) package softened cream cheese

1 (4-ounce) can finely chopped mushrooms, drained

3 finely chopped scallions, divided (set aside 1 chopped scallion for garnish)

1 teaspoon seasoning salt

1 beaten egg

poppy seeds

- Lay out each package of crescent roll dough on a sheet of wax paper and press perforations to seal. This will result in 2 10x15-inch rectangles.
- Mix cream cheese, mushrooms, 2 scallions and salt. Reserve a few mushrooms for garnish.
- Spread ½ of cream cheese mixture on each dough rectangle.
- Roll up jelly-roll-style.
- Wrap in wax paper and freeze at least 1 hour.
- Preheat oven to 375 degrees.
- Slice into ¾-inch pieces and place on greased cookie sheet 2 inches apart.
- Brush with egg and sprinkle with poppy seeds.
- Bake 10-15 minutes. (Allow extra time if dough is still frozen.)
- Garnish with remaining scallions and mushrooms.
- Serve hot.

Yields 4 dozen

Phyllo Spinach and Cheese Bundles

1   (6-ounce) can crabmeat,
     drained
1½ cups shredded Swiss
     cheese, divided
1   (2-ounce) can mushrooms,
     drained
¼   cup crushed crackers
1½ teaspoons dried parsley
½   teaspoon onion powder

1   (10-ounce) package frozen
     chopped spinach, thawed
     and drained
½   teaspoon garlic powder
¼   cup seasoned bread
     crumbs
1   box phyllo pastry
⅛   cup melted butter
     butter-flavored spray

• Preheat oven to 375 degrees.
• Mix crabmeat, ¾ cup Swiss cheese, mushrooms, crackers, parsley and onion powder in food processor to form crabmeat filling. Set aside.
• Mix spinach, ¾ cup Swiss cheese, garlic powder and bread crumbs in food processor to form spinach filling.
• Unfold thawed phyllo dough and lay 3 sheets of phyllo dough on a flat surface.
• Spray each sheet with butter-flavored spray.
• Cut the 3 layers into 20 squares.
• Combine crabmeat and spinach fillings.
• Drop 1 rounded teaspoonful of filling onto each square.
• Bring edges of squares together and place on greased cookie sheet.
• Brush all bundles with melted butter.
• Bake for 15 minutes.
• Can be made ahead and frozen. If cooked frozen, bake for 20 minutes.

Yields 5 dozen

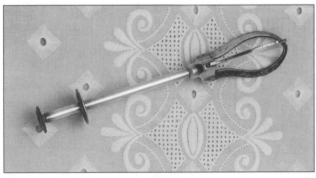

Ice Tongs

Crab Mornay

6	chopped scallions	5	tablespoons dry sherry
½	cup fresh parsley or	1	teaspoon seasoning salt
	¼ cup dried parsley	3	tablespoons sugar
½	cup butter	2	(6-ounce) cans crabmeat,
2	tablespoons flour		drained
2	cups heavy whipping	1	(4-ounce) can mushrooms,
	cream		drained
½	pound grated Swiss cheese		crackers or toasted French
¼	teaspoon red pepper		bread

- Sauté scallions and parsley in butter that has been melted in a large saucepan.
- Stir in flour and slowly add cream; heat until smooth.
- Add cheese and cook on low until cheese is melted.
- Add red pepper, sherry, salt, sugar, crab and mushrooms. Simmer 5 minutes.
- Note: If mixture is too thin, add a bit more cheese and/or flour until desired thickness.
- Serve with crackers or toasted French bread.

Serves 6-8

Hot and Spicy Baked Italian Appetizer

1	pound hot Italian sausage, removed from casing	8	ounces shredded mozzarella cheese
6	eggs	¼	pound diced Genoa salami
1	cup freshly grated Parmesan cheese	½	stick diced pepperoni

- Preheat oven to 350 degrees.
- Brown Italian sausage in saucepan. Drain and set aside.
- Beat eggs well.
- Add Parmesan cheese and mix well.
- Combine mozzarella cheese, salami, pepperoni and sausage with Parmesan cheese mixture
- Bake in 8-inch pan for 25-30 minutes.
- Cut into 1-inch squares.
- Cool before serving.

Yields 4 dozen

Appetizer Tenderloin

2   packages of dry Italian
     salad dressing mix
     red wine vinegar
1   (5- to 7-pound) trimmed
     tenderloin
1   purple onion, sliced into
     rings

2   green peppers, cut into
     strips
1   large jar of capers, drained
2   jars button mushrooms,
     drained
2   cloves of peeled and
     crushed garlic

- Mix dressing according to package directions except use red wine vinegar.
- Pour over meat in large roasting pan.
- Add purple onion rings, green pepper strips, capers, mushrooms and garlic.
- Marinate for 24 hours, turning meat occasionally.
- Preheat oven to 400 degrees.
- Bake for 30-45 minutes or until meat thermometer reaches 140 degrees.
- Slice into thin small pieces.

Serves 50

Mexican Cheese Bread

10 eggs
½   cup all-purpose flour
1   teaspoon baking powder
     dash salt
½   cup melted butter

1   pint creamed cottage
     cheese, run through
     blender
1   (7-ounce) can diced green
     chilies
1   pound shredded Monterey
     Jack cheese

- Preheat oven to 400 degrees.
- Beat eggs.
- Add flour, baking powder and salt.
- Add butter, cottage cheese, chilies and Monterey Jack cheese.
- Mix thoroughly and bake in 9x13-inch baking dish for 15 minutes.
- Reduce heat to 350 degrees and bake 35-40 minutes.
- Cut into squares and serve hot.
- Can be frozen and reheated in foil.

Yields 4 dozen

Blue Cheese Palmiero

1	package puff pastry	1	clove minced garlic
1	(8-ounce) package cream cheese	½	pound bacon, cooked very crisp
1	(4-ounce) package blue cheese	1	beaten egg
		1	tablespoon water

- Preheat oven to 400 degrees.
- Thaw pastry according to package directions.
- Lightly roll out pastry.
- Mix cream cheese, blue cheese and garlic in food processor until smooth.
- Add bacon and turn processor on and off until bacon is crumbled.
- Spread the filling over 2 pastry sheets.
- Start at long edge and roll to the center; roll other edge to meet in the center.
- Roll in plastic wrap and chill at least 20 minutes.
- Slice ⅓- to ½-inch thick and brush top of each slice with egg beaten with water.
- Bake about 10 minutes, until light brown.
- This may be frozen before baking.

Serves 8-10

Hot Buttered Rum

1	pound butter	2	teaspoons ground nutmeg
1	(16-ounce) box brown sugar	1	quart softened vanilla ice cream
1	(16-ounce) box confectioners' sugar	1	jigger rum per serving whipped cream to taste cinnamon sticks
2	teaspoons ground cinnamon		

- Combine butter, brown sugar, confectioners' sugar, cinnamon and nutmeg. Beat until light and fluffy.
- Add ice cream, stirring until well blended.
- Spoon mixture into a 2-quart freezer container and freeze.
- To serve, thaw slightly. Place 3 tablespoons of butter mixture and 1 jigger of rum into a large mug.
- Fill with boiling water and stir well.
- Top with whipped cream and serve with a cinnamon stick.
- Unused butter mixture may be refrozen.

Serves 24

Citrus Fruit Punch

1	gallon orange juice	1	teaspoon almond extract
1	(46-ounce) can pineapple juice	1	cup amaretto liqueur
1	(12-ounce) can apricot juice	1	(750 ml) bottle white wine

- Mix orange juice, pineapple juice, apricot juice, almond extract and amaretto.
- Before serving, add white wine.
- Garnish fruit punch with mint, orange slices and maraschino cherries if serving from a pitcher. Make an ice ring if serving from a punch bowl.
- To make ice ring, boil water needed or use fruit juices. Allow to cool. Arrange decorations in bottom of ring. Pour in just enough water to touch bottom of decorations (maybe ½ of mold depth).
- Freeze thoroughly. Later add remaining liquid and freeze.

Serves 20

Christmas Egg Nog

12 eggs, separated	1 pint whipping cream
12 tablespoons sugar	ground nutmeg or
12 tablespoons blended	cinnamon
whiskey	cream of tartar

- In small bowl, beat egg yolks.
- Gradually add sugar. This should be done slowly.
- Beat until the yolks are thick and lemony in color.
- Add blended whisky.
- In large bowl, beat 1 pint whipping cream. (By adding several teaspoons of confectioners' sugar, you can do this first and refrigerate until needed.)
- In the large bowl, beat 12 egg whites to form stiff peaks. (Add some cream of tartar and this can be refrigerated until needed.)
- In a large punch bowl, fold the egg yolk mixture, whipped cream and egg whites with a wire whisk.
- Sprinkle nutmeg or cinnamon on top and serve.

Yields 12-15 cups

Vodka Punch

1 cup sugar	1 (6-ounce) can frozen 100%
1 cup water	concentrate orange juice
1 liter lemon-lime	1 can water from orange
carbonated drink	juice can
1 (46-ounce) can pineapple	1½ cups vodka
juice	small amount cherry juice
	for color

- Boil sugar and 1 cup water, stirring constantly to make a syrup.
- Add lemon-lime carbonated drink, pineapple juice, orange juice, can of water, vodka and cherry juice.
- Stir until syrup has completely dissolved.
- Pour in 2½-gallon ice cream freezer container and freeze 2-3 days before serving.
- Take out of freezer 1 hour before serving.
- It should become a slush consistency.

Serves 20

Sallie's Margarita

1 (6-ounce) can lime juice	3 ounces Dailey's margarita
1 (6-ounce) can tequila	mix
3 ounces Triple Sec	ice

- Mix lime juice, tequila, Triple Sec and margarita mix.
- Add ice.
- Blend until mixture is slushy.

Serves 4-6

Sangría

½ cup lemon juice	1 bottle port wine
½ cup orange juice	1 (7-ounce) bottle club soda
½ cup sugar	1 cup fruit (any in season)

- Mix lemon juice, orange juice and sugar. Stir until dissolved. This may be done a day ahead.
- At serving time, stir in fruit, wine and soda. Save some fruit to garnish.
- Serve over ice.
- This may be used as a fruit/wine punch or as a refreshing summer drink with meals.

Serves 8

Hot Almond Tea

1 (6-ounce) can frozen	2 cups strong tea
lemonade	½ teaspoon almond flavoring
4 cans water	½ teaspoon vanilla flavoring
½ cup sugar	

- Pour lemonade, water, sugar, tea and almond and vanilla flavorings in saucepan and heat.
- Heat on medium; do not boil.
- More water may be added if too strong or too sweet.
- Serve hot.

Serves 8-10

Hot Cranberry Punch

1   quart apple cider
2   cups cranberry juice

1   cup orange juice
½   cup lemon juice

• Put apple cider and cranberry, orange and lemon juices in bottom of 10-cup percolator.

½-¾ cup sugar
3   sticks cinnamon

1   teaspoon whole cloves
1   teaspoon whole allspice

• Put sugar, cinnamon, cloves and allspice in the basket and perk.

Serves 8-10

Fall Punch

4   cups sugar
2   cups water
1   (12-ounce) can frozen
      orange juice
1   (12-ounce) can frozen
      lemonade

1   (46-ounce) can pineapple
      juice
1   teaspoon vanilla flavoring
1   teaspoon lemon flavoring
1   teaspoon almond flavoring
1   (3-liter) bottle gingerale
1   bag party ice

• Bring sugar and water to a boil.
• Add orange juice, lemonade and pineapple juice. Stir until the frozen juices are melted.
• Stir in vanilla, lemon and almond flavorings.
• Add the gingerale and ice and allow about 3-4 hours to melt some of the ice.

Serves 60

Cran-Lemon Cooler

2 cups water	½ cup lemon juice
½ cup sugar	ice cubes
2 cups cranberry juice	lemon slices

- Combine water and sugar in 1½-quart pitcher.
- Stir until sugar dissolves.
- Add cranberry and lemon juices.
- Chill.
- May spike with vodka if desired.

Serves 6

Champagne is great for any occasion. Mix seasonal fruit purée with champagne. Anyone skipping alcohol can mix fruit purée with seltzer.

Terri's Banana Fruit Slush

6 cups water	1 (46-ounce) can pineapple juice
3 cups sugar	
1 (6-ounce) can frozen lemonade	5 bananas
1 (6-ounce) can frozen orange juice	2 quarts white wine, gingerale, lemon-lime carbonated drink or champagne

- Boil water and sugar until sugar dissolves. Add lemonade and orange and pineapple juices and remove from heat.
- In a blender, mix bananas with ½ cup of juice mixture. Then stir into the remaining juice.
- Freeze in baggies or a large ice cream container.
- To serve, thaw to a slush (45 minutes to 1 hour) and add 1-2 quarts beverage of your choice.

Serves 32 (6-ounce servings)

Fruit Slush

1⅓ cups water
1⅔ cups sugar
2 (11-ounce) cans mandarin oranges and juice
1 (12-ounce) can frozen orange juice

2 (6-ounce) cans frozen lemonade
1 (20-ounce) can crushed pineapple
4 sliced bananas
1 (6-ounce) jar maraschino cherries

- Boil water and sugar to syrup stage and allow to cool.
- Add mandarin oranges, orange juice, lemonade, crushed pineapple, bananas and cherries.
- Mix and freeze in a large container.
- Thaw 1 hour prior to serving.
- Stir with a spoon to make a slush.
- This is a wonderful, refreshing summer treat.

Serves 10-15

Ginger Mint Cooler

1 cup water
½ cup sugar
¼ cup fresh mint leaves
½ cup lemon juice

1 (33.8-ounce) chilled bottle gingerale
green food coloring, optional

- In a small saucepan, combine water, sugar and mint.
- Bring to a boil. Stir until sugar dissolves.
- Strain to remove mint.
- Chill.
- Prior to serving, combine sugar water, lemon juice and gingerale. Add food coloring if desired.

Serves 15

Coffee Punch

1 cup sugar
1 cup water
¼ cup + 2 tablespoons instant
    coffee
3 (13-ounce) cans chilled,
    evaporated milk

1 quart slightly softened
    vanilla ice cream
1 (28-ounce) chilled club
    soda

- Combine sugar, water and coffee in a small saucepan.
- Cook over medium heat, stirring constantly until sugar and coffee dissolve.
- Chill.
- Pour coffee mixture into a punch bowl and stir in evaporated milk.
- Add ice cream and stir until partially melted.
- Add club soda and stir gently.

Yields 1 gallon

Ice rings and ice cubes can easily be given unexpected flair.
Fill ice cube trays or ring molds ½-full with water. Place an edible
flower, a sprig of mint, a fresh berry or even a citrus peel curl on
the water and freeze. Fill with water and freeze until needed.

Hot Holiday Cider

1 (3-inch) cinnamon stick
2 teaspoons whole cloves
1 whole nutmeg
½ gallon apple cider

1 cup sugar
2 cups orange juice
½ cup lemon juice

- Tie cinnamon, cloves and nutmeg in square of cheesecloth.
- Simmer for 15 minutes with apple cider and sugar.
- Remove spice bag and add orange juice and lemon juice.
- Serve hot.

Serves 15

Strasbourg

Soups

Strasbourg

Soups

Strasbourg

Gorham Corporation
Providence, Rhode Island

The <u>Strasbourg</u> pattern, designer unknown, was introduced in 1897 and has remained consistently in demand. The Rococo design recalls the period of Louis XV. The entire handle, with its violin-shaped terminal, is bordered by convex/concave scrolls, the terminal being capped by a shell. In some pieces, the scroll elements extend into bowls and tines.

Gorham Corporation had its start with Jabez Gorham, who began to make jewelry by hand in the early 19th Century. Henry L. Webster joined Gorham in 1831 to make silver spoons. The company expanded dramatically after Gorham's son, John, joined the firm in 1841. John Gorham, an entrepreneur who introduced mechanization into the business and hired talented designers such as George Wilkinson and William Christmas Codman, turned the company into a leading silver manufactory. Along the way, Gorham acquired many other prominent silver companies, including Whiting, Durgin and Alvin. In 1989, Gorham became a subsidiary of Dansk International. In 1990, Dansk was bought by Brown-Forman of Louisville, Kentucky, the maker of Jack Daniels, Canadian Mist, Southern Comfort and other well-known beverages.

Pictured: Bowl made in Maastricht, The Netherlands circa 1724, <u>Strasbourg</u> place setting and American <u>Frontenac</u> soup spoon by Whiting

St. Thomas Fruit Soup

1¾ cups chopped, fresh
   pineapple
¾ cup chopped, ripe
   cantaloupe
¾ cup chopped mango (fresh
   or jarred)
¾ cup apricot nectar
¾ cup sparkling water

1 tablespoon chopped mint
   leaves
whole mint leaves for
   garnish
Optional: add ¼ teaspoon
   almond or coconut
   extract

- Purée pineapple, cantaloupe and mango in blender or food processor.
- With motor running, add apricot nectar, sparkling water and chopped mint.
- Transfer to a covered container and chill at least 4 hours.
- Garnish with mint leaves and serve.
- Can be served partially frozen.

Serves 4

Artichoke Cream Soup

1 (14-ounce) can artichoke
   hearts
2 tablespoons chopped
   onion
4 tablespoons butter, divided
4 tablespoons all-purpose
   flour

½ cup cold milk
3 cups chicken consommé
3 egg yolks
½ cup heavy cream
¼ cup dry white wine
1 teaspoon lemon juice
   salt and pepper to taste

- Drain and chop artichoke hearts. Set aside and cover.
- In a 3-quart saucepan, sauté onion in 1 tablespoon butter until transparent.
- Blend in remaining butter, flour and milk, stirring constantly.
- Add consommé.
- Bring mixture to a boil. Remove 1 cup of hot liquid.
- Combine egg yolks and cream. Stir into reserved hot liquid.
- Add to saucepan, stirring well.
- Add chopped artichoke hearts, wine, lemon juice, salt and pepper.
- Heat thoroughly.

Serves 8

Shrimp Bisque

5 pounds small fresh shrimp	5 cups chicken broth
1 cup butter	7 tablespoons crushed
2½ cups finely chopped onions	tomatoes
2 cups clarified butter	chives for garnish
2 cups flour	salt and pepper to taste
7 cups half-and-half	2 cups dry sherry

- Peel shrimp and lightly sauté in 1 cup butter in a large skillet. Remove shrimp.
- In same skillet, sauté onions in clarified butter until transparent.
- Slowly whisk in flour and cook over low heat 10-15 minutes.
- Heat half-and-half in double boiler until a semi-boil is reached.
- In a large saucepan or soup pot, bring chicken broth to a boil.
- Take off heat and stir half-and-half and broth together in soup pot.
- Add onions and flour mixture and stir together until thick.
- Add tomatoes, shrimp, salt and pepper. Heat thoroughly.
- Add sherry when ready to serve or spoon small amount over each bowl after serving. Garnish.

Serves 20

Emerald Soup

4 cups clarified chicken broth	1 (10-ounce) package frozen broccoli florets
1 package dry leek soup mix	dash hot pepper sauce
4 sprigs chopped parsley	½ cup whipping cream

- In a large saucepan, combine chicken broth and leek soup mix. Bring to a boil.
- Add parsley, broccoli and hot pepper sauce. Cover and boil until broccoli is tender.
- Pour all ingredients in blender or food processor and purée.
- Cool. Stir in cream very slowly.
- Serve hot or cold.
- Good served with Monterey Jack cheese melted on French bread.

Serves 6

Cream of Carrot Soup

8　medium carrots, peeled
　　and sliced ¼-inch thick
2　coarsely chopped, medium
　　onions
2　peeled and sliced celery
　　stalks
3　cups chicken stock, divided

2　peeled and diced, medium
　　potatoes
2　teaspoons salt
¼　teaspoon cayenne pepper
1½ cups half-and-half
1　(17-ounce) jar pimento,
　　drained

- In a large pot, combine carrots, onion, celery, ½ of the chicken stock, potatoes and salt.
- Bring to a boil, then reduce heat, cover and simmer until carrots and potatoes are tender, about 15 minutes.
- Transfer to food processor or blender. Add cayenne pepper.
- With processor or blender running, add remaining ½ of chicken stock and half-and-half. Process until smooth.
- Serve warm or cold. Garnish with diced pimento.

Serves 8

Mushroom Bisque

1　pound chopped fresh
　　mushrooms
1　medium, chopped onion
4　cups chicken broth
7　tablespoons butter or
　　margarine

6　tablespoons flour
3　cups milk
1　cup heavy cream
3　teaspoons dry sherry
　　parsley for garnish

- Simmer mushrooms and onions in broth for about 45 minutes in a large skillet.
- Purée mushroom mixture and return to pot.
- In separate saucepan, melt butter. Blend in flour, stirring constantly for 3 minutes.
- Gradually add milk and simmer until thick, stirring constantly.
- Combine sauce and mushroom mixture.
- Add cream and sherry, stirring to combine.
- Garnish with parsley and serve.

Serves 6-8

Onion, Potato, and Roquefort Soup

2-3 medium, chopped onions
3 tablespoons unsalted butter
1½ large cloves minced garlic
4 medium russet potatoes,
 peeled and chopped

4-5 cups canned, low-salt
 chicken broth
1½ cups whipping cream
½-¾ cup crumbled Roquefort
 cheese
pepper to taste

- Sauté onions in butter over medium heat for about 10 minutes. Add garlic. Do not let garlic brown.
- Add potatoes and chicken broth; simmer until potatoes are tender, about 30 minutes.
- Add whipping cream and cheese. Stir until cheese melts.
- Purée soup in blender in small batches and return to saucepan.
- Thin with additional chicken broth if necessary. Season with pepper.
- May prepare 24 hours ahead. Simmer before serving.

Serves 6-8

Winter White Chili

1 cup chopped onion
2 tablespoons olive oil
2 cloves minced garlic
2½ teaspoons ground cumin
½ teaspoon oregano
4 chicken breasts, cooked,
 skinned, boned and
 chopped
2 cups chicken broth
1 cup water

1 teaspoon lemon pepper
1 (4-ounce) can chopped
 green chilies, undrained
2 tablespoons lemon juice
2 (15-ounce) cans great
 northern beans,
 undrained
2 (7-ounce) cans white
 shoepeg corn, undrained
salt and pepper to taste

- Cook onion in olive oil until transparent in a 4½-quart pot.
- Add garlic and stir.
- Add cumin, oregano, chicken, chicken broth, water, lemon pepper, green chilies, lemon juice, beans, corn, salt and pepper.
- Simmer at least 30 minutes.
- Garnish with fresh chopped cilantro or grated Monterey Jack cheese.

Serves 6-8

Chicken Vegetable Soup

4 cups water	2 tomatoes
4 chicken bouillon cubes	¼ teaspoon Creole seasoning
1 pound boneless, skinless chicken	1 teaspoon dried parsley
	½ teaspoon tarragon
1 cup sliced carrots	¼ teaspoon dried, sweet basil
½ cup chopped celery	1 teaspoon Worcestershire sauce
2 medium Russet potatoes with skin on	hot pepper sauce to taste
1 medium onion	

- Combine water, bouillon and chicken in large saucepan. Simmer until chicken is done.
- Chop chicken into bite-size portions and place back in bouillon mixture.
- Add carrots and celery.
- Chop potatoes, onion and tomatoes into bite-size portions. Add to saucepan.
- Add Creole seasoning, parsley, tarragon, basil, Worcestershire sauce and hot pepper sauce.
- Bring to a boil and then simmer for 1-2 hours.

Serves 6

Harvest Chowder

1 pound ground round	1 (10-ounce) bag frozen corn
4 cups water	2 teaspoons salt
1 (14-ounce) can tomatoes	½ teaspoon pepper
1 cup chopped carrots	1 teaspoon white wine Worcestershire sauce
⅓ cup chopped shallots	
¾ cup uncooked rice	

- Brown meat in large saucepan or Dutch oven.
- Add water, tomatoes, carrots, shallots, rice, corn, salt, pepper and Worcestershire sauce.
- Bring to a vigorous boil, then turn down heat, cover and simmer 1½ hours.
- Best if prepared the day before.

Serves 8 (1-cup servings)

Chicken Jambalaya

½ cup cooking oil	salt, pepper and cayenne pepper to taste
2 cups chopped onion	1 cup cold water
1 cup chopped celery	½ cup chopped green pepper
2 cloves minced garlic	3 tablespoons chopped parsley
2 tablespoons tomato paste	3 cups cooked rice
1 pound browned ground beef	
2 pounds cooked, chopped chicken	

- Heat cooking oil in heavy iron pot.
- Add onions, celery, garlic and tomato paste.
- Cook uncovered over medium heat for 10 minutes.
- Add beef and chicken. Season to taste with salt, pepper and cayenne pepper.
- Add water and cook over medium heat for about 30 minutes, stirring almost constantly.
- Add green pepper and parsley and cook over low heat, uncovered, for 15 minutes.
- Mix in cooked rice and serve.

Serves 10-12

Superb Onion Soup

6 medium, coarsely chopped yellow onions	1 large bay leaf
½ cup peanut oil	4 (10½-ounce) cans beef consommé
1 cup dry red wine	5 cups water
1 teaspoon dried whole thyme	French bread
	6 cups shredded Swiss cheese

- Sauté onion in oil in large Dutch oven until tender.
- Add wine, thyme and bay leaf. Bring to boil and cook 5 minutes.
- Add consommé and water. Reduce heat and simmer, uncovered, for 20 minutes, stirring occasionally.
- Ladle soup into individual baking dishes. Top each with a slice of bread and sprinkle with cheese.
- Place dishes under a broiler for 2-3 minutes or until cheese melts.

Serves 10-12 depending on serving size

Shrimp Gumbo

4	tablespoons bacon drippings or vegetable oil	2	teaspoons salt
7	tablespoons all-purpose flour	½	teaspoon pepper
2	chopped onions	1	teaspoon parsley
1	cup chopped celery	1½	pounds cut okra
1	large, chopped green pepper	1	(28-ounce) can tomatoes
1	clove garlic	1	(15-ounce) can tomato sauce
2	bay leaves	3	tablespoons Worcestershire sauce
	dash red pepper	3-4	pounds shrimp, peeled and deveined

- In large saucepan or soup pot, mix roux by stirring flour into heated oil until golden brown.
- Add chopped onions, celery, green pepper and garlic and stir until well coated with roux mix; cook 15 minutes. Stir often.
- Add bay leaves, red pepper, salt, pepper, parsley, okra, tomatoes, tomato sauce and Worcestershire sauce.
- Simmer 30-40 minutes until okra is done.
- 5 minutes prior to serving, add shrimp. Stir occasionally.
- Serve over steamed rice.
- Best if made a day before. Prepare up to point of adding shrimp. Reheat, add shrimp and heat 5 minutes.

Serves 12

Tomato Citrus Consommé

6	stalks celery	1	cup double-strength beef broth or consommé
½	cup fresh lemon juice		celery salt (optional)
2	cups tomato juice		watercress for garnish
2	cups orange juice		

- In the bowl of food processor, with steel blade, purée celery.
- Add lemon juice and process again.
- Strain mixture and press on pulp to extract all liquid.
- Stir celery mixture, tomato and orange juices and beef consommé.
- Season with celery salt if desired.
- Garnish with watercress and serve hot or cold.

Serves 6

Crock Pot Chili

3   pounds ground beef
½   medium, chopped onion
2   (16-ounce) cans tomatoes
2   (15-ounce) cans light red
      kidney beans

1-1½ ounces Mexene Chili
      Powder*
¼-½ chopped bell pepper
½   cup chopped mushrooms
1   teaspoon mustard
1½ cups water

- In large skillet, brown ground beef and onion. Drain off all fat. Pour into crock pot.
- Cut tomatoes into bite-size pieces and pour with their liquid into crock pot.
- Drain kidney beans and add to tomatoes.
- Add chili powder, peppers and mushrooms.
- Add 1½ cups water. (Crock pot should be almost filled to the top.)
- Cook on low for 8 hours.

* If this is not available, you may substitute any chili powder.

Serves 10

Brunswick Stew

1   (3-pound) chicken
3   pounds pork loin
3   cups canned or fresh
      tomatoes
3   cups cooked, diced
      potatoes
1   cup canned corn niblets

1   (14-ounce) bottle catsup
2   teaspoons hot pepper
      sauce
3   teaspoons Worcestershire
      sauce
3   cups broth from chicken
      and pork

- Fill large pot ¾-full of water and add meat. Bring to boil and slowly simmer until done. Simmer at least 2 hours.
- Take meat from pot, debone and chop into small pieces.
- Pour broth into container for later.
- Put meat back into pot and add tomatoes, potatoes, corn, catsup, hot pepper sauce and Worcestershire sauce; moisten with broth.
- Simmer for 35-40 minutes.

Serves 10

Chantilly

Salads

Chantilly
Salads

Chantilly
Gorham Corporation
Providence, Rhode Island

Chantilly, introduced in 1895, was designed by William Christmas Codman, the famous English designer who joined Gorham in 1891. The design is in the style of 18th Century France and is named after the palace of Chantilly, located outside Paris. The handle is slightly waisted below the terminal and has restrained scroll elements on its margins, both front and back. When introduced originally as The Chantilly, the ornamentation extended down into the margins of the bowls and tines. It was offered in four varieties: bright finish, enamel, Delft enamelled and gilt. The original pieces, which were of heavy weight, hand-finished and expensive, were not well received.

Reintroduced in 1904 with simpler ornamentation and in a grey finish as The New Chantilly, this less expensive version caught on. It eventually became the best-selling silver flatware pattern in the entire world. It is still very popular today.

For a history of Gorham, see the discussion of Strasbourg.

Pictured: English flower or fruit bowl, 1920 American salad fork and spoon serving set with shell bowls and Chantilly place setting

Mint Julep Salad

3 cups cantaloupe balls
3 cups honeydew balls
3 cups blueberries
3 whole cardamom
½ cup honey

½ cup water
½ cup Rosé wine
6 crushed mint leaves
1 tablespoon lemon juice

• Combine cantaloupe balls, honeydew balls and blueberries and chill.
• Peel and crush cardamom. Combine cardamom with honey, water and wine in saucepan and simmer for 5 minutes.
• Add mint leaves and cool.
• Strain into a small bowl. Stir in lemon juice.
• Pour over fruit and mix gently.

Serves 6-8

Mandarin Orange Salad

4 ounces slivered almonds
2 tablespoons sugar
2 (11-ounce) cans drained mandarin oranges
1 head red leaf lettuce, washed and torn into salad-size pieces

1 head green leaf lettuce, washed and torn into salad-size pieces
½ cup chopped scallions
1 cup chopped celery

Dressing

¼ cup red wine vinegar
1 tablespoon sugar
½ cup salad oil

3 drops hot pepper sauce
salt and pepper to taste

• Place almonds and sugar in saucepan over medium heat. Simmer until sugar melts and almonds are coated and candied.
• Combine mandarin oranges, lettuce, scallions and celery and toss.
• Blend vinegar, sugar, oil and pepper sauce for dressing.
• Add salt and pepper to taste.
• Drizzle dressing over salad. Toss to coat and serve immediately.

Serves 6-8

Fruit and Raisin Salad

2	apples	1	cup drained pineapple pieces
1	cup chopped celery	1	cup raisins
½	cup walnut or pecan pieces	½	cup dressing

- Core, peel and cube apples.
- Combine apples with celery, nuts, pineapple and raisins.

Dressing

4	tablespoons butter	½	teaspoon salt
4	tablespoons flour	2	egg yolks
1	cup water	¼	cup vinegar

- Mix butter and flour to form paste and add water.
- Heat on top of double boiler until smooth and thick.
- Add salt and egg yolks.
- Cook until egg yolks thicken. Remove from heat and add vinegar.
- Beat until smooth, and mix ½ cup dressing thoroughly with salad.

Serves 6

Congealed Fresh Vegetable Salad

1	(6-ounce) package lemon or lime gelatin	2	cups diced tomatoes
1½	cups boiling water	1½	cups diced green pepper
1	teaspoon salt	1	cup diced carrots
¼	teaspoon white pepper	½	cup diced scallions
2	tablespoons vinegar	½	teaspoon celery seed
	dash Worcestershire sauce		lettuce leaves (optional)
2	cups cold water		lemon slices (optional)

- Dissolve gelatin in boiling water.
- Add salt, pepper, vinegar and Worcestershire sauce. Stir in cold water.
- Chill until consistency of unbeaten egg white.
- Fold in tomatoes, green pepper, carrots, scallions and celery seed.
- Spoon into 7-cup mold and refrigerate until firm.
- Unmold on lettuce and garnish with lemon slices, if desired.

Serves 12-14

Fruit Salad with Blueberry Dressing

2 cups blueberries	2 cored, chopped red apples
2 peeled and sliced kiwi	2 cored, chopped green
1 bunch green grapes	apples
1 bunch seedless red grapes	lemon juice
1 pint halved strawberries	

Dressing

½ cup blueberry vinegar (or strawberry or raspberry)	1 cup oil

- Prepare fruit and place in oversized bowl, reserving apples.
- Dip apples into lemon juice as you chop, drain on paper towel and add to other fruit.
- Blend vinegar and oil.
- Gently mix fruit and pour dressing over salad or serve on the side.
- Prepare this salad a few hours before serving.

Serves 24

Avocado and Tomato Aspic

2 envelopes unflavored gelatin	12 ounces spicy tomato juice
½ cup water	1 cup chopped celery
6 ounces lemon gelatin	2 peeled and chopped avocados
2½ cups boiling water	¾ cup chopped scallions
¼ cup lemon juice	1 cup peeled and chopped cucumber
2 (10¾-ounce) cans tomato soup	1 cup sliced black olives

- Soak unflavored gelatin in ½ cup water. Add gelatin mixture and lemon gelatin to boiling water. Stir over heat until all is dissolved.
- Remove from heat and add lemon juice, tomato soup and tomato juice.
- Pour into 2-quart mold and cool.
- Add celery, avocados, scallions, cucumber and black olives. Chill until set.
- Garnish suggestions: Top with spoonful of sour cream and fresh sprig of cilantro or parsley.

Serves 16

York's Salad with Feta

¼ cup olive oil
⅛ cup balsamic vinegar
1   bag Italian salad greens

½ cup golden raisins
¼ cup pine nuts
½ square crumbled Feta
     cheese

- Mix olive oil and vinegar.
- Toss with greens, raisins and pine nuts.
- Divide into individual serving bowls.
- Sprinkle with Feta cheese.

Serves 6

Palm Artichoke Salad

1 (10-ounce) can drained
    heart of palm
1 (10-ounce) can drained
    artichoke hearts
1 (4-ounce) jar chopped
    pimento
1 large, thinly sliced red
    onion

1 head washed and torn
    romaine lettuce
1 head washed and torn
    iceberg lettuce
½ cup freshly grated
    Parmesan cheese

Dressing

½ cup olive oil
⅓ cup red wine vinegar

¼ teaspoon freshly ground
     pepper
     salt to taste

- Thinly slice palm hearts and cut artichokes into 6-8 pieces. Wrap in paper towels and gently squeeze.
- Drain all liquid from pimento.
- Mix artichokes, palm hearts, pimento and onion with greens.
- Fill bowl ½-full of salad mixture.
- Sprinkle with ¼ cup cheese. Add remaining salad mixture and top with remaining cheese.
- Cover tightly and chill.
- Whisk together olive oil, vinegar, pepper and salt.
- Pour dressing over salad 10 minutes before serving.

Serves 10-12

Rocky Creek Salad

1	head finely chopped lettuce	1	(12-ounce) jar sliced, marinated artichoke hearts
2	large, sliced purple onions		
3	sliced tomatoes	1	pint jar mayonnaise
1	(16-ounce) jar sliced pickled beets	1	(8-ounce) carton cottage cheese
2	sliced avocados		paprika to taste

- Layer ingredients as follows: ⅓ of lettuce, ½ of purple onion, tomatoes, beets, ⅓ of lettuce, avocados, remaining purple onion, artichoke hearts and remainder of lettuce.
- Mix mayonnaise and cottage cheese together and add as topping to salad.
- Sprinkle with paprika.

Serves 8-10

Salad Radicchio

¼	pound wild greens	3	mandarin oranges (or one 11-ounce can drained mandarin oranges)
1	head radicchio		
1	medium white onion		

Dressing

1	small red delicious apple	1	teaspoon maple syrup
3	tablespoons apple cider vinegar or balsamic vinegar	1	pinch freshly ground white pepper
		2	tablespoons walnut oil
½-1 teaspoon herb salt			

- Rinse and drain greens. Separate and tear radicchio into pieces.
- Peel and chop onion.
- Peel mandarin oranges and seed and halve segments.
- Combine greens, radicchio, onion and oranges in bowl.
- Quarter, core and grate apple.
- Blend apple, vinegar, herb salt, syrup, pepper and oil.
- Toss salad with dressing.
- Mushrooms may be substituted for the oranges.

Serves 6-8

Oriental Surprise Salad

1	pound cooked fresh shrimp, peeled and deveined	1	tablespoon lemon juice
		½	teaspoon curry powder
1	(10-ounce) package cooked and drained frozen green peas	⅛	teaspoon garlic salt
		⅛	teaspoon pepper
1	cup finely chopped celery	1	(3-ounce) can chow mein noodles
½	cup mayonnaise	½	cup salted cashew nuts
			mixed salad greens

- Combine shrimp, peas, celery, mayonnaise, lemon juice, curry powder, salt and pepper.
- Mix well and chill.
- Just before serving, add noodles and nuts. Toss lightly.
- Serve over mixed salad greens.

Serves 4

Olive and Swiss Cheese Salad

8	small scallions, cut in pieces	½	cup olive oil or salad oil
		1	tablespoon vinegar or lemon juice
2	cups stuffed green olives		
6	ounces Gruyère or Swiss cheese	1	tablespoon Dijon mustard
		1	teaspoon black pepper
1	head torn lettuce	1	teaspoon salt

- With metal blade of food processor in place, chop scallions about 5 seconds.
- Insert slicing disk and add olives.
- Insert shredding disc and process cheese.
- Toss in bowl with lettuce.
- Mix oil, vinegar, mustard, pepper and salt together.
- Add to salad and serve.

Serves 8

Salad Niçoise

1 pound well scrubbed new potatoes
2 pounds cooked green beans
10 very ripe Italian plum tomatoes, washed and quartered
1 small peeled and thinly sliced purple onion
½ cup Niçoise olives

¼ cup chopped Italian parsley
⅛ teaspoon salt
1 teaspoon freshly ground pepper
6 shelled and quartered hard-boiled eggs
1½ cups chopped, cooked chicken

- Cook potatoes in boiling salted water until tender, not mushy, about 10 minutes.
- Cool potatoes and cut into quarters. Place in large bowl.
- Add green beans, tomatoes, onion, olives, parsley, salt and pepper.
- Pour dressing over vegetables and gently toss until vegetables are coated.
- Transfer mixture to a large serving platter. Arrange hard-boiled eggs around the edge of the platter.
- Arrange chicken over the salad.
- Drizzle additional dressing and serve at room temperature.

Serves 6-8

Salad Niçoise Dressing

4 tablespoons red wine vinegar
1 teaspoon granulated sugar
½ teaspoon salt
½ teaspoon freshly ground pepper

1 tablespoon prepared Dijon mustard
minced parsley or fresh chives to taste
½ cup olive oil

- Whisk vinegar, sugar, salt, pepper, mustard and herbs in bowl.
- Continue to whisk mixture while slowly adding olive oil until mixture becomes thicker.
- Adjust seasoning as needed and cover until ready to use. Dressing is best if used immediately.

Yields ¾ cup

Fusilli and Chicken Pasta Salad

1 (16-ounce) package cooked fusilli
1 (7-ounce) jar pimento, drained
1 (12-ounce) jar marinated artichoke hearts
½ cup sliced black olives
4 chopped tomatoes

6 boneless mesquite chicken breasts, cooked and chopped
¼ cup olive oil
2 tablespoons wine vinegar
2 tablespoons fresh parsley
2 tablespoons fresh basil

- Mix pasta, pimento, artichoke hearts, olives, tomatoes and chicken.
- Blend olive oil, vinegar, parsley and basil.
- Pour over pasta mixture and toss.
- Chill before serving.

Serves 6

Oriental Chicken Salad

½ package fried rice sticks
2 whole chicken breasts, cooked and cut into bite-size pieces

1 bunch diced scallions
½ cup sliced and toasted almonds
½ cup toasted sesame seeds

Dressing

¼ cup sugar
2 teaspoons salt
1 teaspoon monosodium glutamate

½ teaspoon pepper
¼ cup wine vinegar
½ cup salad oil

- Fry rice sticks by breaking off small handfuls and putting them into hot oil. They will puff up immediately. Remove from oil and drain on paper towels.
- Combine rice sticks, chicken, scallions, almonds and sesame seeds in a large bowl.
- Combine sugar, salt, monosodium glutamate, pepper, vinegar and salad oil in a blender.
- Just before serving, toss dressing with salad.

Serves 6-8

How Did You Make This Salad?

1 head iceberg lettuce	6 halved cherry tomatoes
1 head green leaf lettuce	3 tablespoons fresh chives
1 cup diced, grilled or oven roasted zucchini	2 ounces crumbled blue cheese
2 cups cooked chicken (may substitute tuna or shrimp)	1 cup toasted croutons

- Mix together lettuce, zucchini, chicken, tomatoes, chives, blue cheese and croutons.
- Suggested additions or substitutions include cooked and crumbled bacon, avocado, grilled eggplant, spinach or hard-boiled eggs.

Dressing

1 teaspoon salt	2 tablespoons lemon juice
½ cup sugar	½ teaspoon Worcestershire sauce
¼ teaspoon black pepper	1 clove minced garlic
½ teaspoon paprika	½ cup olive oil
½ teaspoon dry mustard	
½ cup herb vinegar spiced with tarragon or basil	

- Mix salt, sugar, pepper, paprika, mustard, vinegar, lemon juice, Worcestershire sauce, garlic and oil together.
- Drizzle dressing over salad just before serving.

Serves 8

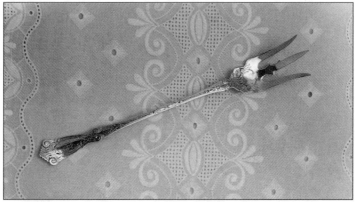

American Lettuce Serving Fork

Robin's California Salad

1	head red leaf lettuce or green leaf spinach	6	slices cooked and crumbled bacon
1	head romaine lettuce	3	sliced, fresh Italian tomatoes
1	diced avocado	4	chopped scallions
2	cups diced, cooked chicken (may substitute cooked shrimp or tuna)	3	tablespoons crumbled blue cheese
		1	cup toasted croutons
		½	cup Parmesan cheese

- Toss red leaf and romaine lettuce, avocado, chicken, bacon, tomatoes, scallions and blue cheese.
- Top with croutons and Parmesan cheese and drizzle with dressing.

Dressing

1	teaspoon salt	½	cup tarragon vinegar
½	teaspoon sugar	2	tablespoons lemon juice
¼	teaspoon black pepper	½	teaspoon Worcestershire sauce
½	teaspoon paprika	⅛	teaspoon garlic or 1 clove minced garlic
½	teaspoon dry mustard		
½	cup olive oil		

- Mix salt, sugar, pepper, paprika and mustard together, and whisk in oil, vinegar, lemon juice, Worcestershire sauce and garlic.
- Can refrigerate any remaining dressing.

Serves 8

Greek Salad Dressing

1	cup olive oil	1	large clove minced garlic
½	cup red wine vinegar	¼	teaspoon salt
1	tablespoon sugar	½	teaspoon oregano

- Make this dressing 24 hours before serving.
- Combine oil, vinegar, sugar, garlic, salt and oregano and refrigerate.
- Add to salad just before serving.

Yields 1½ cups

Blue Cheese and Chicken Salad

⅔ cup chopped walnuts
2½ cups cooked chicken or
    turkey
1 cup thinly sliced celery

¼ cup thinly sliced scallions
seedless grapes
pineapple chunks
lettuce

- Blanch walnuts in boiling water for 3 minutes and drain well.
- Spread walnuts in shallow baking pan and toast at 350 degrees for 10-12 minutes or until golden brown.
- Mix together walnuts, chicken, celery, scallions, grapes and pineapple.

Dressing

1 cup mayonnaise
2 tablespoons crumbled blue
    cheese

1 tablespoon lemon juice
½ teaspoon salt
¼ teaspoon curry powder

- Mix together mayonnaise, cheese, lemon juice, salt and curry powder, blending well.
- Add dressing to chicken mixture and chill.
- Serve on a bed of lettuce.

Serves 8

Chicken Pasta Salad

1 fryer chicken
1 (12-ounce) package
    corkscrew pasta
6-8 chopped scallions
1 (15-ounce) can sliced black
    olives
¼ cup white vinegar
¼ cup salad oil

½ cup olive oil
2 tablespoons water
1 package Italian salad
    dressing mix
1 teaspoon salt
¼ cup freshly grated
    Parmesan cheese

- Boil chicken and cut into chunks.
- Cook pasta and drain.
- Mix pasta and chicken.
- Add scallions and olives.
- Mix vinegar, oils, water and salad dressing mix together. Add salt and Parmesan cheese.
- Refrigerate.

Serves 8

Shrimp Vermicelli Salad

1 (12-ounce) package
 vermicelli
1½ pounds cooked and peeled
 fresh shrimp
3 chopped hard-boiled eggs
1½ cups chopped scallions
1 cup chopped dill pickle
¼ cup minced parsley
1 chopped small green
 pepper
1 (2-ounce) jar drained,
 sliced pimento

1 cup mayonnaise
1 (8-ounce) carton sour
 cream
¼ cup lemon juice
2 tablespoons prepared
 mustard
1 teaspoon celery seed
1 teaspoon salt
¼ teaspoon pepper
½ cup Parmesan cheese

• Break vermicelli into pieces. Cook according to package directions and drain.
• Add shrimp, eggs, scallions, pickles, parsley, green pepper and pimento. Set aside.
• Combine mayonnaise with sour cream, lemon juice, mustard, celery seed, salt, pepper and Parmesan cheese and stir well. Pour over shrimp mixture and toss gently.
• Cover and chill for 2 hours.

Serves 8

Crunchy Celery Pasta Salad

1 (12-ounce) package
 spaghetti
1 tablespoon seasoning salt
3 tablespoons lemon juice
4 tablespoons oil
1 medium, chopped bell
 pepper

1 medium, chopped onion
½ cup chopped celery
1 (4-ounce) jar sliced
 pimento
1 cup grated longhorn Colby
 Jack cheese

• Break spaghetti into 1-inch pieces. Cook as directed on package, rinse and drain.
• Mix salt, lemon juice, oil, pepper, onion, celery and pimento.
• Combine with cooked spaghetti and marinate overnight.
• Top with cheese before serving.

Serves 8-10

Cold Marinated Beef Salad

2 tablespoons oil
1 pound sliced or quartered
   mushrooms
3 tablespoons lemon juice
   salt and pepper to taste
4 tablespoons olive oil
4 tablespoons red wine
   vinegar
2 cloves crushed garlic
¼ teaspoon chervil
¼ teaspoon thyme

¼ teaspoon basil
1½ pounds broiled steak or
   3-4 cups cooked beef cut
   into julienne strips
   (seasoned well)
1 pint halved cherry
   tomatoes
1 head lettuce
½ cup grated Asiago cheese
   chopped parsley for
   garnish

- Heat oil in skillet. Add mushrooms, lemon juice, salt and pepper. (May add garlic if desired.) Cook until mushrooms are tender. Set aside.
- In a large bowl, beat olive oil, vinegar, garlic, chervil, thyme, basil, salt and pepper. Add beef, tomatoes and mushrooms.
- Toss lightly to coat and arrange on bed of lettuce. Sprinkle with Asiago cheese and parsley.
- This is a good recipe for leftover steak and beef tenderloin.

Serves 6

Marinated Wild Rice Salad

1 box long-grain and wild
   rice
1 cup chopped celery
½ cup toasted pecans
   juice of 1 lemon

2 tablespoons white wine
   vinegar
⅓ cup olive oil
   freshly ground pepper

- Cook rice according to directions, omitting the butter. Let cool to room temperature.
- Add chopped celery and toasted pecans.
- In a small bowl, mix lemon juice, vinegar and oil.
- Add a lot of pepper, to taste. Adjust lemon and pepper as needed.
- Toss with rice and chill.

Serves 8-10

French Kick Pasta

1   (8-ounce) bag favorite pasta
1   medium chopped tomato
1   chopped bell pepper

1   (8-ounce) can sliced black
      olives
1   small chopped onion
2   cups raw broccoli florets

• Cook pasta according to package directions, rinse and cool.
• Combine tomato, pepper, olives, onion and broccoli and toss with dressing.

Dressing

1   cup oil
¼   cup vinegar
1½ teaspoons salt
⅛   teaspoon pepper
¼   teaspoon paprika

¾   teaspoon Worcestershire
      sauce
2   tablespoons ketchup
2   teaspoons lemon juice
¼   teaspoon garlic salt

• Combine oil, vinegar, salt, pepper, paprika, Worcestershire sauce, ketchup, lemon juice and salt and mix well.
• Serve over pasta.

Serves 8

New Potato Salad

1½ pounds new potatoes
½   cup melted butter
5   chopped scallions
½   teaspoon dry mustard
1   teaspoon celery seed

1   teaspoon dill weed
¼   cup light mayonnaise
1   tablespoon horseradish
1   tablespoon lemon juice

• Boil potatoes in salted water.
• Chill and quarter potatoes.
• Add butter, scallions, dry mustard, celery seed and dill.
• Mix mayonnaise, horseradish and lemon juice together.
• Fold mayonnaise mixture into potatoes.

Serves 10-12

Italian Pasta Salad

1   pound vegetable rotini
1   chopped green pepper
3-4 chopped or sliced carrots
1   (8-ounce) can sliced black
    olives
1   medium, chopped purple
    onion
1   medium, chopped red
    pepper

1   pint halved cherry
    tomatoes
1   package Italian dressing
    mix
    freshly ground pepper
¼   cup freshly grated
    Parmesan cheese

• Cook pasta according to package directions, omitting salt. Rinse with cold water.
• Combine pasta with green pepper, carrots, olives, onion, red pepper and tomatoes.
• Mix Italian dressing according to package directions.
• Pour dressing over pasta and vegetables. Generously grind pepper on top.
• Toss with Parmesan cheese.

Serves 8

Nana's Green Pasta Salad

1   pound package tri-color
    rotini pasta
2   bell peppers
2   tomatoes
¾   cup olive oil
4   tablespoons lemon juice
4   tablespoons red wine
    vinegar

2   teaspoons dried oregano
    salt and pepper to taste
1   large can sliced black olives
½   cup chopped scallions
1   pound crumbled Feta
    cheese
3   tablespoons dill weed

• Boil pasta, drain and rinse.
• Slice bell pepper lengthwise.
• Cut tomatoes into chunks.
• Whisk oil, lemon juice, vinegar, oregano, salt and pepper together and pour over pasta.
• Allow to stand and absorb dressing.
• Add peppers, tomatoes, olives, scallions, Feta cheese and dill weed. Mix well and serve.

Serves 6

Party Antipasto Pasta Salad

1 (9-ounce) package fresh cheese tortellini	1 pint fresh cherry tomatoes
1 (6-ounce) can ripe olives	1 pint fresh mushrooms
1 (15-ounce) can garbanzo beans	1 cup julienned carrots
2 (14-ounce) cans artichoke hearts	1 cup julienned green pepper
	1 cup julienned yellow squash

- Cook tortellini, omitting salt and oil. Drain.
- Pit and drain olives. Drain garbanzo beans. Drain and quarter artichoke hearts.
- Cut tomatoes and mushrooms in halves or quarters.
- Combine tortellini, olives, beans, artichoke hearts, tomatoes, carrots, pepper and squash in a bowl.

Dressing

⅔ cup chicken broth	2 teaspoons sugar
¼ cup white wine vinegar	2 teaspoons Dijon mustard
1 (2-ounce) jar diced pimento, drained	2 teaspoons olive oil
1 teaspoon Italian seasoning	½ teaspoon garlic powder
2 tablespoons lemon juice	½ teaspoon salt

- Whisk broth, vinegar, pimento, Italian seasoning, lemon juice, sugar, mustard, olive oil, garlic powder and salt together.
- Pour dressing over vegetables and pasta.

Serves 10

Broccoli with Cashew Sauce

½ cup coarsely chopped cashews	2 tablespoons honey
3 tablespoons unsalted butter	2 bunches fresh, steamed, chopped broccoli

- Sauté nuts in butter over low heat for 5 minutes.
- Add honey and cook 1 minute, stirring constantly.
- Pour hot sauce over broccoli and toss to coat.

Serves 8

Black Bean and Chicken Pasta Salad

6   ounces medium pasta
      shells
1   cup chicken
1   (10-ounce) can black beans
1½ cups shredded red cabbage
⅓   cup chopped sweet red
      pepper
3   tablespoons olive oil

3   tablespoons lemon juice
2   tablespoons finely chopped
      fresh dill
2   tablespoons Dijon mustard
½   teaspoon salt
¼   teaspoon pepper
      lettuce leaves
2   tomatoes, cut into wedges

• Cook pasta shells according to package directions and drain and rinse.
• Cut chicken into chunks and mix with drained and rinsed beans.
• Add cabbage and red pepper.
• Mix together oil, lemon juice, dill, mustard, salt and pepper.
• Add shells and dressing to chicken mixture.
• Toss gently to blend and chill.
• Serve on lettuce with tomato wedges as garnish.

Serves 8

Zucchini and Rice Salad with Assorted Greens

½   cup olive oil
2   tablespoons rice or white
      wine vinegar
2   cloves pressed garlic
1   tablespoon soy sauce
½   teaspoon freshly ground
      pepper
3   cups cooked white rice
¼   pound fresh spinach leaves

4   chopped scallions
1   small julienned zucchini
½   cup chopped celery
¼   cup slivered almonds
      assorted brightly colored
      salad greens
2   tablespoons chopped
      parsley

• Place olive oil, vinegar, garlic, soy sauce and pepper in a jar and shake to mix well.
• Pour mixture over hot rice and toss. Cover and chill until serving time.
• Prior to serving, combine rice and spinach, scallions, zucchini, celery and almonds. Season to taste.
• Spoon the rice mixture on a bed of greens and sprinkle with parsley. Serve immediately.

Serves 6-8

Chilled Asparagus with Dill Mustard Sauce

1	pound thin, fresh asparagus	2	heaping tablespoons freshly minced chives
1	cup firm, plain yogurt		salt and pepper to taste
¼	cup mayonnaise		salad greens
⅓	cup Dijon mustard		cherry tomatoes
2	heaping tablespoons freshly minced dill		

- Snap the very bottom tiplets from asparagus spears, leaving spears long.
- Steam asparagus until tender and crisp.
- Run asparagus under cold water and drain.
- Combine yogurt, mayonnaise, mustard, dill, chives, salt and pepper and mix well.
- Place asparagus in a long shallow dish, pour dressing over and chill for 1 hour.
- Serve on a bed of greens and garnish with cherry tomatoes.
- If fresh herbs are unavailable, 1 teaspoon dried herbs may be substituted per 1 tablespoon fresh herbs.

Serves 4

Black Bean Salad

2	(15-ounce) cans rinsed and drained black beans	1	medium, chopped purple onion
2	(15-ounce) cans drained shoepeg corn	½	cup sugar
1	large jar drained pimentos	¼	cup white vinegar
1	large, chopped green bell pepper	¼	cup red wine vinegar
3	stalks chopped celery	¼	cup olive oil
		1	teaspoon salt
		½	teaspoon pepper

- Mix beans, corn, pimentos, bell pepper, celery and onion in a large salad bowl.
- Combine sugar, vinegars, oil, salt and pepper and mix well.
- Pour dressing over vegetables and coat well.
- Cover and marinate at least 3 hours in the refrigerator.
- Will keep refrigerated for several days.
- Drain before serving.

Serves 8-10

Fresh Tomato Salad

salad greens
4 medium ripe tomatoes,
   sliced vertically
3 tablespoons chopped
   scallions
3 tablespoons chopped
   parsley

pinch sugar
   salt and pepper to taste
2 tablespoons red wine
   vinegar
⅛ teaspoon salt
¼ teaspoon dry mustard
6 tablespoons salad oil

- Line plate with salad greens and arrange tomato slices on top.
- Sprinkle with scallions, parsley, sugar, salt and pepper.
- Shake together vinegar, salt, mustard and oil. Pour over tomatoes.
- Refrigerate at least 30 minutes before serving.
- Easy, delicious and a good way to use those tomatoes in the summer.

Serves 4-6

Crunchy Coleslaw

2 tablespoons butter
2 packages Ramen beef
   noodles
1-1½ pounds coleslaw
½ cup sunflower kernels

½ cup toasted, slivered
   almonds
1 bunch chopped scallions
2 shredded carrots

- Break up noodles and sauté in butter until golden brown.
- Mix noodles with coleslaw, sunflower kernels, almonds, scallions and carrots.
- Just before serving, drizzle dressing over the salad.

Dressing

½-¾ cup olive oil
¼-½ cup sugar
⅓ cup balsamic or white
   vinegar

2 packages seasoning from
   Ramen beef noodles

- To prepare dressing, mix oil, sugar, vinegar and seasoning packages together and refrigerate overnight.

Serves 6-8

Spinach Poppy Seed Salad

2 pounds fresh spinach	½ pound crisply fried bacon,
3 hard-boiled eggs	crumbled
	8-10 sliced fresh mushrooms

- Wash, tear and stem spinach.
- Slice cooled hard-boiled eggs.
- Combine spinach, bacon, eggs and mushrooms in bowl.
- Toss with Bama's Poppy Seed Dressing.

Serves 8-10

Bama's Poppy Seed Dressing

⅔ cup sugar	1 teaspoon salt
½ cup vinegar	1 small onion
2 teaspoons (rounded) dry	1½ cups well chilled salad oil
mustard	2 tablespoons poppy seed

- Blend sugar, vinegar, mustard, salt, onion and oil in a blender (not food processor) until thick and milky, and onion is puréed.
- Add poppy seed.
- Mix well and serve over fruit or salad.

Yields 2 cups

California Dressing for Spinach Salad

1 egg	½ cup apple cider vinegar
¾ cup sugar	½ teaspoon salt
½ teaspoon dry mustard	

- In a saucepan, beat egg until frothy.
- Add sugar, mustard, vinegar and salt and heat to boiling, stirring constantly.
- Cool and refrigerate.
- Top spinach salad with boiled egg slices and bacon bits. Top with dressing when ready to serve.

Yields ¾ cup

Caboose Dressing

1-2 cloves garlic
½ cup cider vinegar
1 teaspoon paprika
1 teaspoon salt
1 medium chopped onion

½ cup sugar
1 cup salad oil
1 (10¾-ounce) can
   Campbell's tomato soup

• Drop 1 or 2 cloves garlic into jar or bottle.
• Mix vinegar, paprika, salt, onion, sugar, oil and soup in a blender. Mix well.
• Pour mixture into jar with garlic and refrigerate.

Yields 3 cups

Our family has enjoyed this delicious dressing since my mother was given the recipe by a neighbor in Ohio in the 40's. The neighbor's husband worked for the railroad - hence the name.

Strawberry Spinach Salad

10 ounces fresh spinach   1 pound fresh strawberries

Dressing
¼ cup sugar
   juice of 1 large lemon

1 egg yolk
4-6 tablespoons vegetable oil

• Rinse, drain, stem and coarsely tear spinach.
• Hull and halve strawberries.
• Layer spinach and strawberries with strawberries ending on top.
• Refrigerate 3-4 hours to enable spinach to absorb strawberry flavor.
• Combine sugar and lemon juice in mixing bowl. Whisk until most of sugar is dissolved.
• Blend in egg yolk. Add oil, one tablespoon at a time, whisking constantly until dressing is thick and creamy.
• Cover and refrigerate.
• When ready to serve, whisk dressing and pour over salad. Toss gently.

Serves 6-10

Best Dressing

1	tablespoon prepared Dijon mustard	½	teaspoon freshly ground pepper
4	tablespoons red wine vinegar		minced parsley and/or snipped chives to taste
1	teaspoon sugar	½	cup olive oil
½	teaspoon salt	1½	tablespoons sour cream

- Measure mustard into a bowl. Whisk in vinegar, sugar, salt, pepper and herbs.
- Continue to whisk, adding oil until mixture thickens.
- Add sour cream and continue to whisk.
- Adjust seasoning as needed to taste and cover until ready to use. Whisk if necessary before serving.
- Dressing will keep up to 2 weeks in refrigerator, but is best if used after 1 hour.

Yields ¾ cup

Heavenly Fruit Dip

½	cup sugar	1	tablespoon butter or margarine
2	tablespoons flour		
1	cup pineapple juice	1	cup whipping cream, whipped
1	medium, beaten egg		

- Combine sugar, flour, pineapple juice, egg and margarine in a heavy saucepan.
- Cook over medium heat, stirring constantly 2-3 minutes after it comes to a low boil or until smooth.
- Let cool completely.
- Fold in whipping cream.
- Chill and store in refrigerator.
- Serve with fresh fruit.
- Can be made the night before.

Yields 3 cups

Old Master

Entrees

Old Master
Towle Silversmiths
Newburyport, Massachusetts

Old Master was introduced in 1942 and was one of the last flatware patterns to be introduced before the silverware industry essentially shut down for the duration of World War II. Designed by Harold E. Nock, it has been one of the most desired patterns by buyers of American silver. The design, with its waisted terminal and scrolled borders, echoes the style of 18th Century France.

Towle Silversmiths traces its origins back to the Moulton family of Newbury, later Newburyport, Massachusetts. This family produced a distinguished succession of silversmiths, one of which, Joseph, sold the firm around 1860 to Towle & Jones. Towle & Jones became A. F. Towle & Son in 1873, Towle Manufacturing Company in 1882 and eventually the Towle Silversmiths. Wallace-International acquired Towle in 1990.

Pictured: French tray, three-piece English carving set and Old Master place setting

Stuffed Châteaubriand with Madeira Sauce

1   (4-pound) châteaubriand
     (or tenderloin)
⅓   pound finely chopped
     fresh mushrooms
½   small, finely chopped
     onion
3   tablespoons butter

½   teaspoon flour
2   tablespoons brandy
1   (4- or 5-ounce) can pâté
     with truffles
¾   pound bacon
     twine

- Prepare charcoal grill. Medium-hot coals are needed. A gas or electric grill does not give best results.
- Make a 1¾-inch deep cut down the center on top of the meat to form a pocket. Do not cut through the 2 ends of the meat.
- In a heavy 8- to 10-inch skillet, sauté mushrooms and onion in butter over medium heat for 3-5 minutes. Sprinkle flour over mixture and add brandy, stirring until slightly thickened. Simmer 5 minutes, stirring frequently.
- Add pâté, stirring to blend. Remove skillet from heat and cool slightly. Stuff mushroom mixture into the cavity in the meat.
- Layer strips of bacon lengthwise over the top and bottom of the meat, encasing the meat in the bacon. Tie the meat and bacon securely with all-cotton twine every few inches to hold in the mushroom mixture.
- Barbecue for about 45 minutes or until meat thermometer registers 130 degrees. Turn to ensure even cooking.
- Remove from the grill to warm serving platter. Remove strings and bacon. Slice thinly.
- Serve with Madeira Sauce Merrill.

Serves 8

Madeira Sauce Merrill

3 tablespoons butter	¼ cup Madeira wine
1½ tablespoons flour	1 teaspoon Worcestershire
¾ cup beef stock	sauce
1 teaspoon thickener	⅓ cup sautéed, minced, fresh
(cornstarch)	mushrooms

- Melt butter in heavy 1½- to 2-quart saucepan over medium-low heat. Add flour, stirring well and cook 5 minutes.
- Add beef stock, gravy thickener, wine and Worcestershire sauce. Cook over medium heat 3 minutes. Stir in mushrooms.
- Serve with châteaubriand.
- Sauce may be prepared up to a day ahead and reheated prior to serving.

Yields 1 cup

Beef Broccoli Wellington

1 pound ground beef	9 ounces cooked and drained
4 ounces mozzarella cheese	broccoli
½ cup chopped onion	2 cans crescent rolls
½ cup sour cream	1 beaten egg
¼ teaspoon salt	poppy seeds (optional)
¼ teaspoon pepper	

- Preheat oven to 375 degrees.
- In medium skillet, brown meat and drain.
- Stir in cheese, onion, sour cream, salt, pepper and broccoli. Simmer 10 minutes.
- Separate dough into 4 rectangles. Press perforations to seal. Overlap long sides of 2 rectangles; press firmly to seal.
- On ungreased cookie sheet, press or roll into a 13x7-inch rectangle. Spoon meat mixture in the center of the dough. Bring long edges to the center of filling, slightly overlapping. Pinch edges and ends to seal.
- Repeat with remaining rectangles. Brush with beaten egg and sprinkle with poppy seeds.
- Bake 18-22 minutes or until brown.
- Variation: Add mushrooms after browning meat.

Serves 6

Châteaubriand with Cognac-Mustard Sauce

1	(4- to 5-pound) beef tenderloin roast	2	tablespoons cognac
4	cloves slivered garlic	2	tablespoons Dijon mustard
3	tablespoons olive oil	4	tablespoons minced, fresh parsley
4	minced shallots	8	tablespoons unsalted
1	tablespoon unsalted butter		butter, cut in 8 pieces
2	cups beef stock		

- Preheat oven to 450 degrees.
- Using the tip of a sharp knife, cut slits into the meat and push the garlic slivers completely in.
- Brush meat well with oil. Heat remaining oil in heavy skillet on medium-high. (If necessary, cut tenderloin into 2 pieces to fit into pan.)
- Quickly brown the meat on all sides. Place the meat on a rack in a roasting pan and roast to desired doneness, about 30 minutes for rare.
- In skillet used for browning meat, sauté shallots in 1 tablespoon butter until soft. Set aside until meat is desired doneness.
- When meat is done, remove from heat and tent with foil. Pour excess fat from roasting pan.
- In skillet, add beef stock to shallots. Scrape pan to loosen any browned bits. Boil until reduced by ½.
- Add cognac and boil 1 minute. Reduce heat to low.
- Whisk in mustard, then parsley.
- Whisk in butter 1 piece at a time.
- Season with salt and pepper to taste.
- Slice beef ½-inch thick. Arrange slices on platter and spoon sauce over meat.

Serves 8

Broccoli Beef Pie

2   cups chopped, fresh
    broccoli
1   pound ground beef
1   (4-ounce) can mushroom
    pieces, drained
2½ cups shredded Cheddar
    cheese, divided
⅓   cup chopped onion
2   cups biscuit mix

½   cup water
4   eggs
    dash of pepper
½   cup milk
¼   teaspoon salt
¼   teaspoon garlic salt
½   cup grated Parmesan
    cheese

- Preheat oven to 350 degrees.
- In saucepan, cook broccoli in small amount of boiling water for 5 minutes. Drain.
- Brown ground beef in a large skillet, stirring to crumble. Drain.
- Stir in mushrooms, 1½ cups Cheddar cheese and onion. Remove from heat.
- Combine biscuit mix and water in mixing bowl. Stir to form soft dough. Add ½ cup Cheddar cheese and stir until blended.
- Flour hands and pat dough into a greased 13x9x2-inch baking dish. Spread dough halfway up the sides of the dish.
- Spoon meat mixture over dough. Top with broccoli
- Combine eggs, pepper, milk, salt and garlic salt. Beat well. Pour over broccoli.
- Combine Parmesan cheese and remaining ½ cup Cheddar cheese. Sprinkle over casserole.
- Bake uncovered for 35 minutes or until knife comes out clean.

Serves 8

Phil's Favorite Stir-fry

2   teaspoons sherry
⅛   teaspoon pepper
2   teaspoons soy sauce
½   teaspoon salt
½   teaspoon sugar
¾   cup water, divided
2   teaspoons cornstarch

¾   pound broccoli
½   pound flank steak
4   tablespoons peanut oil,
     divided
1   thinly sliced onion
3   cups cooked rice

- Mix sherry, pepper, soy sauce, salt and sugar with ½ cup water. Set aside.
- Mix cornstarch with remaining ¼ cup water and set aside.
- Remove broccoli florets from stems. Cut stems diagonally. Reserve.
- Slice flank steak across grain into 1½-inch strips.
- Heat 2 tablespoons oil in uncovered wok or electric skillet heated to 300 degrees. Add broccoli stalk slices and onions. Cover; cook 2 minutes.
- Add florets and cook 2 minutes more. Remove broccoli and onions to a plate and keep warm.
- Add remaining 2 tablespoons oil to wok. Heat to 375 degrees and add meat. Stir-fry 2 minutes.
- Return broccoli and onions to wok. Add cornstarch mixture and sherry mixture. Stir until thickened.
- Serve with rice.

Serves 2-4

American Roast Holder for Carving

Flank Steaks

4 pounds flank steak
1 clove garlic
¼ cup salad oil
2 tablespoons lemon juice
2 tablespoons soy sauce

2 tablespoons chopped
   onion
1 teaspoon black pepper
1 teaspoon celery seed
1 tablespoon meat tenderizer

- Clean steaks of fat.
- Crush garlic. Mix with salad oil, lemon juice, soy sauce, onions, pepper, celery seed and meat tenderizer.
- Place steaks in flat container and pour oil mixture over. Pierce meat with a fork.
- Cover and refrigerate overnight. Turn meat. Refrigerate until ready to grill.
- Grill to desired doneness, about 10 minutes on each side.
- Slice on the diagonal and serve.

Serves 6-8

Marinated Eye of Round Roast

¼ cup oil
2½ tablespoons lemon pepper
½ cup wine vinegar
½ cup lemon juice

½ cup soy sauce
½ cup Worcestershire sauce
1 (5-pound) eye of round
   roast

- Combine oil, lemon pepper, vinegar, lemon juice, soy sauce and Worcestershire sauce.
- Marinate roast in oil mixture 1-3 days, turning daily.
- Preheat oven to 250 degrees.
- In a Dutch oven, bake uncovered in marinade 2-3 hours, depending on degree of doneness desired.
- Serve hot or cold.

Serves 10-15 (depending on thickness of slices)

Entrecôte Marchand de Vin
(Steak in Wine Sauce)

1 **inch-thick sirloin, T-bone, New York strip, round steak or filet mignon**	1 **tablespoon olive oil**
	6 **chopped shallots**
	10 **sliced mushrooms**
¼ **cup butter**	1 **cup red wine**

- Trim fat and remove bones from steak.
- Melt butter in a large skillet, and add olive oil. When bubbly and turning brown, add meat.
- Cook 5 minutes on each side. Remove meat to platter and slice.
- Add shallots and mushrooms to butter. When browned, add wine and simmer a few minutes.
- Pour over sliced steak.

Servings depend on amount of steak

Oriental Beef Tenderloin

½ **cup teriyaki sauce**	2 **tablespoons honey**
¼ **cup oil**	1-2 **cloves crushed garlic**
2 **teaspoons herbed or rice vinegar**	4-6 **pounds tenderloin of beef freshly ground black pepper**
1 **teaspoon ground ginger**	

- Up to 2 days before serving, prepare marinade. Blend teriyaki sauce, oil, vinegar, ginger, honey and garlic. Pour over meat, cover and refrigerate.
- Remove meat from marinade and season generously with pepper.
- Grill tenderloin on gas grill on high heat 3 minutes. Turn meat, and cook 3 more minutes. Reduce heat to low and cook 12 additional minutes.
- Remove from grill. Slice diagonally and serve.

Serves 4-6

Sicilian Meat Roll

2 pounds ground beef
2 beaten eggs
1 cup soft bread crumbs
½ cup tomato juice
¼ cup chopped, fresh parsley
1 teaspoon salt
1 teaspoon oregano
½ teaspoon pepper

2 cloves minced garlic
8 thin slices proscuitto ham
1½ cups shredded mozzarella cheese
½ cup grated Parmesan cheese
6 ounces sliced mozzarella cheese

- Preheat oven to 350 degrees.
- Combine beef, eggs, bread crumbs, tomato juice, parsley, salt, oregano, pepper and garlic.
- Place mixture on large sheet of foil and shape into a 10x12-inch rectangle.
- Arrange proscuitto slices on top of beef mixture. Sprinkle with grated cheeses. Leave an inch or so on long edge for sealing.
- Carefully roll, starting with short end, like a jelly roll. Place seam side down in baking dish.
- Bake 1 hour and 15 minutes.
- Place cheese slices on top of meat roll. Bake 5 minutes longer.
- Allow to stand 10 minutes before slicing.

Serves 8

Italian Breaded Chicken

1 cup Italian bread crumbs
¼ cup Parmesan cheese
¼ cup chopped, blanched almonds
2 teaspoons minced parsley
1 teaspoon salt

¼ teaspoon dried thyme
⅛ teaspoon pepper
½ cup butter
1 clove crushed garlic
1 (3-pound) fryer, cut in pieces

- Preheat oven to 375 degrees.
- Combine bread crumbs, Parmesan cheese, almonds, parsley, salt, thyme and pepper.
- In a small saucepan, melt butter and add garlic.
- Dip chicken pieces in garlic butter and then in dry mix.
- Bake uncovered for 45 minutes.

Serves 4

Short Ribs and Rice

3   pounds short ribs
1½ teaspoons salt, divided
½   teaspoon pepper
    all-purpose flour
1   tablespoon butter
2   (1-pound) cans stewed
    tomatoes

⅓   cup snipped celery leaves
¼   cup chopped green pepper
¼   teaspoon chili powder
⅓   cup seedless raisins
1   tablespoon lemon juice
6   cups cooked rice
4-6 thin slices lemon

- Cut ribs into serving pieces. Salt and pepper ribs, then coat with flour.
- Melt butter in Dutch oven. Brown ribs on all sides.
- Add tomatoes, celery leaves, green pepper, 1 teaspoon salt and chili powder. Simmer, covered, 2-2½ hours, until ribs are 'fork tender'.
- Stir in raisins and lemon juice. Simmer covered for 10 minutes.
- Serve over rice. Garnish with lemon slices that have been twisted.

Serves 6

Paupiettes de Veau

6   veal cutlets
½   pound ground veal
2   tablespoons minced onion
5   tablespoons browned,
    ground smoked sausage
4   tablespoons fresh bread
    crumbs
½   teaspoon ground pepper

4   tablespoons chopped
    mushrooms
¼   cup flour
½   cup butter
1   tablespoon cooking oil
½   cup sliced mushrooms
1   cup white wine
    twine

- Trim and pound cutlets.
- Mix ground veal, onions, sausage, bread crumbs, pepper and chopped mushrooms.
- Place heaping tablespoonful of this mixture on each veal cutlet. Roll and tie with twine.
- Dredge cutlets in flour. Heat butter and oil in skillet.
- Brown cutlets.
- Add sliced mushrooms and wine and simmer 45 minutes.

Serves 6

Veal Piccata

¼ cup flour	2 tablespoons fresh lemon juice
½ teaspoon pepper	½ cup white wine
½ teaspoon garlic salt	1 thinly sliced lemon
½ pound veal scallopini	2 tablespoons capers
½ cup butter	finely minced parsley to garnish
2 tablespoons olive oil	
½ pound sliced fresh mushrooms	

- Combine flour, pepper and garlic salt and coat veal.
- Heat butter and oil in skillet. Brown veal.
- Add mushrooms, lemon juice and white wine to the skillet.
- Cover skillet and simmer on low for 5-10 minutes.
- Add lemon slices and capers and heat thoroughly.
- Garnish with parsley and serve.

Serves 2

Lemon Dijon Chicken

1 sliced onion	1 cup dry white wine
2 cloves peeled and crushed garlic	1 teaspoon Dijon mustard
8 boneless chicken breasts	4-5 lemons or limes
1 cup teriyaki sauce	¼ cup fresh rosemary or tarragon

- Preheat oven to 350 degrees.
- Sauté onion and garlic.
- Place chicken in a deep roasting pan and top with onions and garlic.
- In a separate bowl, mix teriyaki sauce, wine, mustard and juice of lemons.
- Pour over chicken.
- Place chopped fresh herbs on top.
- Bake for 1 hour.
- This is wonderful served over rice.

Serves 8

Purse de Poulet

4 Tyson skinless, boneless
   chicken breast halves
2 tablespoons dried chopped
   basil, divided
1 teaspoon salt, divided
2 teaspoons white pepper,
   divided
1 tablespoon olive oil
1½ cups water

   juice of one lemon
½ cup diced Vidalia onion
2 tablespoons butter
1 cup grated Asiago cheese
1 (16-ounce) package filo
   dough
   melted butter
4 fresh chives about
   12 inches long
1 egg

- Preheat oven to 350 degrees
- Sprinkle both sides of chicken with 1 tablespoon basil, ½ teaspoon salt, and 1 teaspoon white pepper.
- Heat olive oil in skillet on medium high heat. Add chicken and cook on each side, just until chicken is browned.
- Pour water and lemon juice over chicken. Cover and simmer for 15 minutes or until done.
- Remove chicken from skillet and cut into small pieces; set aside.
- Heat 2 tablespoons butter in skillet on medium high heat until melted. Add onion and sauté until almost transparent.
- Combine chicken, sautéed onion, cheese and remaining 1 tablespoon basil, ½ teaspoon salt and 1 teaspoon white pepper.
- Brush four sheets of filo dough with melted butter. Stack these on top of each other. Cut in half, horizontally. Place 2 tablespoons chicken mixture in center of filo and bring 4 corners together to form a bundle. Tie a chive around each bundle to seal.
- Brush a mixture of 1 egg and ¼ cup of water beaten well, over pastries.
- Bake at 350 degrees for 15 minutes or until golden brown.

Serves 8

Chicken Enchiladas

1	whole chicken	1	teaspoon sugar
1	cup chopped onion	1	teaspoon ground cumin
1	clove minced garlic	½	teaspoon salt
2	tablespoons butter	½	teaspoon crushed oregano
1	(16-ounce) can chopped tomatoes	½	teaspoon crushed basil
		12	cornmeal tortillas
1	(8-ounce) can tomato sauce	¾	cup sour cream
1	(4½-ounce) can chopped green chilies	2½	cups (10 ounces) shredded Monterey Jack cheese

- Cook, skin and bone a whole chicken. Pull meat off in thin strips.
- Preheat oven to 350 degrees.
- In a saucepan, cook onion and garlic in butter until onion is transparent.
- Add tomatoes, tomato sauce, ½ can of chilies, sugar, cumin, salt, oregano and basil. Bring to a boil.
- Reduce heat and simmer uncovered for 20 minutes. Remove from heat.
- Dip each tortilla into tomato mixture.
- Place strips of chicken and 2 tablespoons of shredded cheese on each tortilla, roll up and place seam side down in a 13x9-inch baking dish that has been coated with cooking spray.
- Blend sour cream into remaining tomato mixture and pour over tortillas.
- Sprinkle with remaining cheese.
- Cover and bake for 40 minutes.

Serves 4-6

Chicken Cacciatore

1	(27½-ounce) jar low-fat, tomato-based pasta sauce	2	pounds boned and skinned chicken breasts
½	cup Burgundy or dry red wine	1	teaspoon dried Italian seasoning
1	bell pepper, cut in 1-inch pieces	½	teaspoon salt
1	onion, cut in 1-inch pieces	¼	teaspoon pepper
		2	mashed garlic cloves
		6	cups cooked fettuccine

- Combine pasta sauce, wine, bell pepper and onion in Dutch oven.
- Add chicken and bring to a boil. Cover, reduce heat and simmer for 1 hour or until chicken is tender.
- Remove chicken and let cool.
- Cut chicken in bite-size pieces; set aside.
- Add Italian seasoning, salt, pepper and garlic and cook uncovered over medium heat for 15 minutes, stirring frequently.
- Add chicken and cook until heated.
- Serve over fettuccine.

Serves 6

Petti de Pollo Mimosa

6	skinless, boneless chicken breasts	3	tablespoons butter
2	eggs	3	tablespoons olive oil
1½	teaspoons salt	6	slices Proscuitto ham
¼	teaspoon white pepper	6	slices mozzarella cheese
½	cup flour	½	cup chicken broth
		¼	cup white wine

- Pound chicken breasts to flatten.
- Beat eggs with salt and pepper.
- Dip chicken breasts in egg, then in flour.
- In a large saucepan, melt butter and oil.
- Brown chicken about 8 minutes on each side.
- Place a ham slice on each breast.
- Top with cheese slice.
- Add chicken broth and wine.
- Cover and simmer for 5 minutes.

Serves 6

Stuffed Chicken Breasts

6   skinned and boned chicken breasts
¼   teaspoon salt
1   (6-ounce) package sliced Swiss cheese
6   thin slices ham
¼   cup flour
⅓   cup butter

2   tablespoons instant chicken bouillon
1   cup water, divided
1   (3-ounce) can sliced mushrooms
2   tablespoons flour
⅓   cup sauterne wine

- Preheat oven to 350 degrees.
- Place chicken breasts on cutting board and pound chicken to make ¼-inch-thick cutlets. Sprinkle with salt.
- Place a cheese slice and a ham slice on each piece of chicken.
- Tuck in sides, roll and fasten well with toothpicks.
- Coat chicken with ¼ cup flour.
- Heat butter in skillet and brown chicken in butter.
- Remove chicken to 11x7x1½-inch baking dish.
- Combine ½ cup water, bouillon and mushrooms in same skillet. Heat, stirring to remove crusty bits from skillet.
- Pour over chicken.
- Cover and bake for 1 hour.
- To make sauce, blend 2 tablespoons flour with ½ cup water and add wine.
- Stir liquid into baking pan and cook, stirring until thickened.
- Remove chicken to serving platter and pour small amount of sauce over chicken.

Serves 6

Meat Servings

8 ounces per person if boneless
10-12 ounces per person with bone

Champagne Chicken

3	tablespoons all-purpose flour	2	tablespoons orange-flavored liqueur
1	teaspoon salt	¾	cup dry champagne
6	skinned and boned chicken breasts	1	cup chicken bouillon
2	tablespoons butter, divided	1	cup sliced, fresh mushrooms
1	tablespoon cooking oil	½	cup whipping cream

- Preheat oven to 350 degrees.
- Combine flour and salt.
- Coat chicken breasts in flour mixture.
- Heat 1 tablespoon butter and oil in a large skillet.
- Add chicken and cook for 5 minutes on each side.
- Place chicken in a 9x9x2-inch baking pan and bake uncovered for 20 minutes.
- Pour fat from skillet and add orange-flavored liqueur, champagne and bouillon and bring to a simmer.
- Add chicken and simmer, uncovered, for 20 minutes or until tender.
- Cook mushrooms in 1 tablespoon butter. Then add mushrooms and cream to chicken.
- Spoon into serving dish.

Serves 6

Lime Marinated Chicken

6-8	hickory wood chips for the grill	1	clove garlic
½	cup white wine vinegar	4	skinless, boneless chicken breasts
½	cup soy sauce	1	large onion, halved and then quartered
2	tablespoons lime juice		

- Soak hickory wood chips in water.
- Combine vinegar, soy sauce, lime juice and garlic in food processor. Process for 10 seconds.
- Place chicken in a 13x9x2-inch pan and add onion.
- Pour vinegar mixture over chicken and cover.
- Refrigerate overnight, turning once.
- Grill chicken using hickory wood chips.

Serves 4

Grilled Chicken Pesto and Tortellini

1 cup commercial pesto sauce	6 skinless, boneless chicken breasts
½ cup mayonnaise	4 sliced Roma tomatoes
¼ cup finely chopped red onion	1 thinly sliced red pepper
	1 thinly sliced yellow pepper
1 (20-ounce) package tortellini	1 thinly sliced green pepper

- Mix pesto, mayonnaise and onion.
- Cook pasta according to package directions.
- Toss with ¾ of the pesto mix. Use remainder of sauce to coat the chicken.
- Grill chicken breasts until cooked, thoroughly basting with sauce.
- After turning chicken breasts once, add sliced peppers and tomatoes to the grill to cook the remainder of the time.
- Slice cooked chicken in thin pieces.
- Place pasta on a large platter, top with sliced chicken and arrange peppers on top. Encircle with tomatoes.

Serves 6

Chicken Oregano

6-8 boned chicken breasts	2 diced, fresh tomatoes
1 teaspoon salt	1 large can mushrooms, undrained
¼ cup vegetable oil	
1 medium, chopped onion	½ teaspoon pepper
1 minced garlic clove	2 tablespoons oregano

- Salt chicken on both sides.
- In a heavy or electric skillet, brown chicken in oil on both sides over medium heat.
- Add onion and garlic; cover and cook for 3 minutes.
- Add tomatoes, mushrooms and juice, pepper and oregano.
- Cover and cook slowly for 30 minutes.
- This makes a good gravy over rice or creamed potatoes.

Serves 6-8

Gourmet Mustard Chicken

8	boneless chicken breasts	½	teaspoon cayenne pepper
6	tablespoons Dijon mustard	½	cup melted butter
1	tablespoon thyme	2	tablespoons oil
1	teaspoon black pepper	6	croissants

• Preheat oven to 350 degrees.
• Pound chicken breasts to flatten them.
• Combine mustard, thyme, black pepper and cayenne pepper.
• Add ½ of the melted butter and 1 tablespoon of the oil.
• Make bread crumbs by lightly toasting croissants. Let cool and put in blender and pulse until mixture is very fine. Set aside.
• Coat chicken with mustard mixture and then roll in bread crumbs.
• Place coated chicken on greased baking sheet.
• Pour the rest of the butter and oil over the chicken.
• Bake for 30 minutes.

Serves 8

Baked Chicken Delight

1½	cups sour cream	1½	teaspoons pepper
4	tablespoons lemon juice	6	skinless, boneless chicken breasts
2	teaspoons celery salt		
4	minced garlic cloves	2	cups Italian-style bread crumbs
1	teaspoon paprika		
1	tablespoon Worcestershire sauce	¼	cup melted butter

• Combine sour cream, lemon juice, celery salt, garlic, paprika, Worcestershire sauce and pepper.
• Place chicken breasts in a large bowl and marinate in sour cream mixture overnight.
• Preheat oven to 350 degrees.
• Roll each chicken breast in Italian-style bread crumbs.
• Arrange in a single layer in a 9x13x2-inch baking dish.
• Spoon melted butter over chicken breasts.
• Bake uncovered for 1 hour.

Serves 6

Elegant Chicken and Crab

6	skinless, boned chicken breasts	3	tablespoons flour
2½	cups water	¼	teaspoon salt
¼	cup sliced onion	¼	teaspoon pepper
3	teaspoons chicken bouillon	½	cup dry white wine
1	stalk celery	2	beaten egg yolks
½	cup sliced, fresh mushrooms	1	pound crabmeat
¼	cup chopped scallions	½	cup heavy cream, whipped
3	tablespoons butter	½	cup freshly grated Parmesan cheese
			paprika to garnish

- Cook chicken in water with sliced onion, bouillon and celery. Strain stock and reserve 1½ cups.
- Preheat oven to 350 degrees.
- Place chicken in bottom of 13x9x2-inch baking dish.
- Sauté mushrooms and chopped scallions in butter until tender.
- Blend in flour, salt and pepper. Gradually add reserved broth and wine and cook until mixture thickens. Stir constantly.
- Add a small amount of hot mixture to egg yolks and blend thoroughly. Return to hot mixture and cook for 2 minutes. Remove from heat.
- Stir in crabmeat and gently fold in whipped cream.
- Pour sauce over chicken in baking dish.
- Sprinkle with cheese and paprika.
- Bake for 30 minutes.

Serves 6

Chicken Stock Hints

- Save chicken backs and wing tips in zipper-type freezer bag until you have a full bag. Make stock by your favorite recipe. Pour completed stock into 8-ounce styrofoam cups, cover tops with foil and stand cups in muffin pans to keep upright. Freeze completely and label as 1 cup chicken stock and date. This way you will always have chicken stock on hand.
- Do not throw away smaller amounts of stock. Pour into ice cube tray to freeze. One ice cube block = 1½ tablespoons of liquid. Store cubes in zipper freezer bags. Label and date.
- Cook rice, grits, couscous or barley in chicken stock for extra flavor.
- Use chicken stock instead of milk in mashed potatoes.

Chicken with Artichoke Hearts

¼ teaspoon pepper
¼ teaspoon paprika
6 chicken breasts
   vegetable cooking spray
1 minced garlic clove
1 cup chopped onion
½ teaspoon rosemary
½ teaspoon dried whole
   thyme

¼ teaspoon salt
¼ cup dry white wine
1 large chopped tomato
1 (10-ounce) can drained
   artichoke hearts
½ cup plain, low-fat yogurt, at
   room temperature
1 tablespoon cornstarch

- Combine pepper and paprika and sprinkle over chicken.
- Coat skillet with vegetable cooking spray.
- Place chicken in skillet and cook over medium heat for 5 minutes, turning once.
- Combine garlic, onion, rosemary, thyme, salt, wine and tomato in medium bowl. Stir well and pour over chicken.
- Cover and simmer for 10 minutes.
- Add artichokes, cover and simmer additional 5 minutes.
- Remove chicken to serving dish and keep warm.
- Combine yogurt and cornstarch in a small bowl.
- Slowly add yogurt mixture to skillet, at medium heat, stirring constantly. Do not let mixture boil.
- Pour over chicken.

Serves 6

Scalloped Chicken Casserole

4½ tablespoons butter
9   tablespoons flour
3   cups chicken broth
2¼ cups milk
2¼ teaspoons salt
⅜   teaspoon pepper
2   cups cooked rice

2-3 cups diced chicken
⅛   teaspoon paprika
1   (2-ounce) jar pimentos
¾   cup slivered, blanched
     almonds
1   cup cooked mushrooms
     buttered bread crumbs

- Preheat oven to 350 degrees.
- To make gravy, melt butter and stir in flour and blend.
- Add chicken broth and milk, stirring constantly until thickened.
- Add salt and pepper. Set aside.
- Add ½–1 cup broth to rice and mix; set aside.
- Butter a large casserole dish.
- Place a layer of rice on bottom; add a layer of chicken.
- Cover with gravy.
- Sprinkle with paprika, pimento, almonds and mushrooms.
- Repeat layers, beginning with rice.
- Top with buttered bread crumbs.
- Bake 30 minutes.

Serves 6

Fabulous Pork Tenderloin

1   cup vegetable or olive oil
⅓   cup freshly squeezed
     lemon juice
⅔   cup minced, fresh parsley
12-14 crushed cloves of garlic

2   tablespoons salt
1   tablespoon coarsely
     cracked pepper
3-5 pounds pork tenderloin

- Mix oil, lemon juice, parsley, garlic, salt and pepper.
- Marinate pork tenderloin with oil mixture in ziplock bag or sealed tightly in casserole with plastic wrap.
- Drain off marinade and grill meat to desired doneness.

Serves 6-10

Pork Medallions in Mustard Sauce

3 tablespoons vegetable oil	¼ teaspoon black pepper
¼ cup + 1 tablespoon prepared coarse-grain mustard, divided	¼ cup dry white wine
	4 pork tenderloins
¾ teaspoon salt, divided	1¾ cups whipping cream
	⅛ teaspoon white pepper

- Combine vegetable oil, 1 tablespoon mustard, ½ teaspoon salt, pepper and wine.
- Rub on pork tenderloins. Place tenderloins in large ziplock bag and refrigerate 6-8 hours.
- Grill tenderloins.
- To make mustard sauce, heat whipping cream in heavy saucepan, stirring often, for about 15 minutes. Do not boil. It will reduce to about 1¼ cups.
- Stir in ¼ cup mustard, ¼ teaspoon salt and white pepper; heat 1 minute.
- Serve on top of pork tenderloins or as a side sauce.

Serves 6-8

Pork Tenderloins with Orange-Pepper Sauce

12 ounces pork tenderloin	¾ teaspoon coarsely ground black pepper
3 tablespoons flour	
2 tablespoons margarine or butter	⅓ cup dry white wine
	1 tablespoon grated orange peel
¼ cup chopped scallions	
	⅔ cup orange juice

- Preheat oven to 200 degrees.
- Prepare pork by cutting into ½-inch slices, then pounding between 2 sheets of wax paper until about ¼-inch thick. Dust lightly with flour.
- In a wide skillet, melt margarine over medium-high heat; add pork, turning once, until browned on both sides. Remove to another ovenproof pan; keep warm in a 200-degree oven.
- Add scallions and pepper to drippings in pan. Cook, stirring occasionally, until the scallions wilt. Add wine, orange peel and orange juice. Bring to a boil. Stir frequently.
- Cook until reduced to ½ cup. Pour sauce over pork tenderloin and serve.

Serves 4

Pork Tenderloin with Apples

2	boneless pork tenderloins, about 1¾ pounds	2	peeled and quartered Granny Smith apples
	salt and freshly ground pepper	½	cup chopped onion
		2	tablespoons red wine vinegar
3	tablespoons flour		
2	teaspoons ground cumin	½	cup chicken broth
2	tablespoons vegetable oil	2	tablespoons honey
		1	tablespoon tomato paste

- Season pork with salt and pepper. Blend flour with cumin and dredge meat in mixture.
- Heat oil in heavy skillet over medium-high heat. Brown meat on all sides.
- Drain excess fat from skillet and place apples and onions around meat. Cook and stir for 4 minutes. Add vinegar, broth, honey and tomato paste. Simmer, stirring.
- Lower heat, cover pan tightly and cook about 20 minutes.
- Slice pork; arrange apples and onions around meat on platter and spoon sauce over all.

Serves 4-6

Pork Chops L'Orange

6	center-cut pork chops, trimmed	1	large, sliced onion
		1	large clove minced garlic
¼	cup flour	1	cup orange liqueur
2	tablespoons butter	½	cup sour cream
1	tablespoon salt	1	medium, peeled, and thinly sliced orange
¼	teaspoon pepper		

- Coat pork chops with flour. Melt butter in heavy skillet; brown chops on both sides.
- Sprinkle with salt and pepper.
- Add onions, garlic and orange liqueur.
- Simmer, covered, for 45 minutes or until chops are tender. Remove chops to heated platter.
- Reduce heat. Reduce liquid until slightly thickened. Mix in sour cream. Cook until heated through.
- Spoon sauce over chops. Arrange orange slices over all. Serve immediately.

Serves 6

Medallions of Pork with Riesling Sauce

1   (12-ounce) pork
    tenderloin, cut into
    1-inch thick rounds
    salt and pepper
    all-purpose flour
4   tablespoons unsalted
    butter, divided
1   medium, thinly sliced
    onion
3   cloves minced garlic
½   cup dry Riesling wine
½   cup raisins

3   tablespoons balsamic
    vinegar or red wine
    vinegar
1   tablespoon + 2 teaspoons
    drained capers
1½ teaspoons minced, fresh
    thyme
1½ teaspoons minced, fresh
    oregano
4   tablespoons chilled,
    unsalted butter, cut into
    pieces
¼   cup toasted pine nuts

- Season pork with salt and pepper. Coat in flour; shake off excess.
- Melt 2 tablespoons butter in a heavy large skillet over medium-high heat.
- Add onion and garlic and sauté until golden brown, about 5 minutes. Transfer to bowl. Melt remaining 2 tablespoons butter in same skillet over medium-high heat.
- Add pork and sauté about 4 minutes per side for medium. Transfer pork to plate. Tent with foil to keep warm.
- Add onion mixture, wine, raisins, vinegar, capers, thyme and oregano to same skillet and boil until sauce thickens, about 4 minutes.
- Add pork to skillet and heat thoroughly.
- Divide pork among plates.
- Add 4 tablespoons chilled butter to sauce in skillet and whisk until just melted. Stir in pine nuts.
- Spoon sauce over pork and serve.

Serves 4

Pecan-Crusted Pork

24 ounces pork loin (sliced ½-inch thick)	½ teaspoon pepper
½ cup Chablis	¾ cup dry bread crumbs
1 teaspoon dry mustard	¾ cup finely chopped pecans
water	¾ cup unbleached all-purpose flour
1 egg	4 tablespoons vegetable oil
1 egg white	sliced scallions
4 tablespoons Dijon mustard	

- Marinate pork loin overnight in mixture of Chablis, dry mustard and enough water to cover loin. Turn once.
- The next day remove and dry chops and discard marinade.
- Place meat between 2 sheets of wax paper and pound with a meat mallet to ¼-inch thickness.
- Combine egg and egg white; mix well.
- Add mustard and pepper to egg mixture.
- In a separate bowl, combine bread crumbs and pecans.
- Coat chops with flour, then dip in egg mixture and coat with crumb mixture.
- Cook in oil in skillet over medium heat, about 8 minutes, turning once.
- Top with sliced scallions.

Serves 8

Cuban Pork Roast

1 cup orange juice	1 clove minced garlic
½ cup lemon juice	1 pork tenderloin
½ cup brown sugar	extra brown sugar

- Combine orange juice, lemon juice, brown sugar and garlic.
- Marinate pork loin in this mixture overnight or 8 hours.
- Bake at 350 degrees until done. (A 5-pound pork loin takes approximately 2 hours.)
- Sprinkle extra brown sugar over meat.
- Slice and serve.

Serves 2

Roast Pork with Cherry Sauce

1 (4-pound) boneless pork loin roast	1¼ cups sugar
1 teaspoon salt	¼ cup white vinegar
1 teaspoon pepper	¼ cup cornstarch
1 teaspoon sage	¼ teaspoon almond flavoring
12 whole cloves	1 tablespoon lemon juice
1 stick cinnamon	1 tablespoon butter
1 (16-ounce) can water-packed red cherries	curly lettuce
	lemon wedges

- Preheat oven to 325 degrees.
- Sprinkle roast with salt, pepper and sage. Place fat side up, in shallow roasting pan on a rack. Insert meat thermometer.
- Bake 1½-2 hours, or until thermometer registers 160 degrees. Remove from oven.
- Tie cloves and cinnamon in cheesecloth bag.
- Drain cherries, reserving liquid. Add water to make liquid ¾ cup.
- Combine ½ cup cherry liquid, sugar, vinegar and spice bag. Bring to a boil and simmer 10 minutes. Remove spice bag.
- Combine cornstarch and ¼ cup cherry liquid and stir into hot liquid. Stir constantly 1 minute until it thickens.
- Add cherries, almond flavoring, lemon juice and butter.
- Serve roast on a platter lined with curly lettuce and garnish with lemon curls and wedges. Sauce is served on the side.

Serves 8-10

American "Bone Cover"

Crown Roast of Fresh Pork
with Apple-Mustard Sauce

2	teaspoons salt	1	(16-rib) crown roast of
1	teaspoon freshly ground pepper		fresh pork (about 8 pounds)
1½	teaspoons dried thyme		vegetable oil for rubbing
1½	teaspoons dried, crumbled sage		pork

- In small bowl, combine salt, pepper, thyme and sage. Rub onto pork. Chill pork, covered, overnight.
- Rub pork with vegetable oil on the next day.
- Preheat oven to 450 degrees.
- Cover bottom of lightly oiled, shallow roasting pan with heavy duty foil. Lightly oil top of foil.
- Place pork on foil and roast for 20 minutes.
- Reduce heat to 325 degrees and roast for 1 hour and 45 minutes, or until meat thermometer registers 160 degrees for medium-well done, 170 degrees for well done meat.
- Transfer pork to a platter. Serve with apple-mustard sauce on side.

Serves 8-12

Apple-Mustard Sauce

½	cup cider vinegar	½	cup finely chopped, dried apples
½	cup dry white wine		
1	cup apple cider	1	tablespoon cornstarch
1	cup chicken broth, divided	2	tablespoons Dijon mustard
5	tablespoons firmly packed dark brown sugar		salt and pepper to taste

- In medium saucepan, combine vinegar, wine, cider, ¾ cup of chicken broth, brown sugar and apples.
- Bring to a boil, stirring occasionally. Simmer 5 minutes.
- In small bowl, whisk together cornstarch and remaining ¼ cup chicken broth. Add to apple mixture, continue whisking.
- Bring to a boil and simmer 2 minutes. Remove from heat and whisk in mustard, salt and pepper.

Yields 3½ cups

Ham and Fruit Roll-Ups

4	ripe bananas
½	pound thinly sliced, boiled ham
1	(8-ounce) can pineapple chunks, undrained
1	teaspoon malt vinegar

6	ounces brown sugar, divided
1	teaspoon cinnamon
1	teaspoon cornstarch
1	cup cold, black coffee
2	teaspoons rum extract parsley for garnish

- Preheat oven to 350 degrees.
- Peel bananas and halve lengthwise. Roll each banana piece in a slice of ham.
- Place rolls close together in a shallow, greased baking dish. Bake 30 minutes.
- While baking, prepare sauce. Drain pineapple juice in saucepan, reserving fruit. Add vinegar and 4 ounces of brown sugar. Bring to a boil and boil 5 minutes.
- Blend cinnamon and cornstarch in coffee. Add to mixture in saucepan. Cook until thickened and clear.
- Add pineapple and rum extract. Spoon over ham rolls. Sprinkle with remaining brown sugar.
- Bake 30 more minutes.
- Garnish with parsley.

Serves 4

Excellent for a light poolside supper. Serve with a spicy couscous, fresh asparagus and tiny muffins. Also great for brunch.

Pasta Proscuitto and Vegetables
with a Winter Tomato Sauce

¾ cup finely chopped onion
¼ cup finely chopped carrot
¼ cup finely chopped celery
2 large cloves minced garlic
½ tablespoon oregano
½ tablespoon basil
1 bay leaf
  salt and pepper to taste
1½ tablespoons olive oil
⅓ cup dry red wine
1½ tablespoons tomato paste
1 (28- or 32-ounce) can
  whole Italian tomatoes,
  undrained
1 pound asparagus, sliced on
  the diagonal

½ cup sliced, unpeeled
  zucchini
1 cup snow peas
½ cup chopped, unpeeled
  yellow squash
¼ pound finely chopped
  proscuitto
½ cup butter, divided
½ pound mushrooms, whole
  or quartered
½ pound fresh linguine
¾ cup heavy cream
⅓ cup freshly grated
  Parmesan cheese
  salt and pepper to taste
¼ cup toasted pine nuts

- In a heavy saucepan, cook onion, carrots, celery, garlic, oregano, basil, bay leaf, salt and pepper in oil over moderate heat. Stir until vegetables are softened and add wine. Add tomato paste and tomatoes with juice.
- Simmer sauce, covered, over low heat 35 minutes, stirring occasionally.
- Simmer sauce, uncovered, 15-20 minutes or until thickened. Discard bay leaf. Set sauce aside.
- Sauce may be made up to 2 days in advance and kept covered and chilled.
- Steam asparagus, zucchini, snow peas and squash separately until tender and crisp. Set aside.
- Sauté proscuitto briefly in a small amount of butter. Set aside.
- Sauté mushrooms in ¼ cup of butter. Add reserve vegetables and simmer just until hot. Do not let vegetables overcook.
- Cook pasta until tender. Add ¼ cup melted butter, cream, Parmesan cheese, proscuitto, salt and pepper and mix gently.
- Place pasta mixture in the center of a large platter. Surround with the vegetables and top vegetables with the tomato sauce. Sprinkle with toasted pine nuts.

Serves 4-5

Ham Loaf

1¼ pounds ground, center ham
¾ pound sausage
¾ cup saltine cracker crumbs
2 eggs
½ cup milk

black pepper to taste
¾ cup brown sugar
¼ cup water
1½ teaspoons dry mustard
¼ cup vinegar

- Preheat oven to 350 degrees.
- Mix ham, sausage, cracker crumbs, eggs, milk and pepper.
- Bake in a loaf pan, covered with foil, for 1 hour.
- Combine brown sugar, water, dry mustard and vinegar in a saucepan. Bring to boil and heat 10 minutes. Pour over loaf.
- Return to oven for 30 more minutes, cooking uncovered.

Serves 6

This timeless recipe has been served at bridal luncheons in Dothan for many years. Ham Loaf was originally featured in our League's *Ginger Bread House Cookbook,* published in 1961.

Laura's Barbecue Shrimp

5 pounds unpeeled shrimp
2 cups melted butter
½ cup pepper

16 ounces Italian salad dressing
juice of 4 lemons

- Preheat oven to 350 degrees.
- Combine shrimp, butter, pepper, dressing and lemon juice, and put in large roaster.
- Roast covered for 45 minutes. Stir every 15 minutes.

Serves 6

Coquilles St. Marie

6	tablespoons butter, divided	1	cup heavy cream
4	tablespoons flour	⅛	teaspoon cayenne pepper
1	pound scallops (quarter deep sea scallops)	½	teaspoon salt white pepper to taste
3	tablespoons finely chopped shallots	1	cup peeled, diced tomatoes
½	cup dry white wine	3	tablespoons Parmesan cheese
1	cup sliced, fresh mushrooms	3	tablespoons bread crumbs

- Melt 3 tablespoons butter.
- Add butter to flour to make a beurre manié. Set aside.
- Wash and drain scallops. Set them aside.
- In a large skillet, melt 1 tablespoon butter and sauté shallots until soft.
- Add the wine to the sautéed shallots. Raise the heat and cook until wine is reduced by ½.
- Add the scallops and mushrooms. Cook over high heat for 3-4 minutes.
- Reduce heat and slowly add the cream, stirring constantly.
- Season with cayenne, salt and pepper.
- Add the beurre manié by dollops. Stir until thickened.
- Add tomatoes and stir gently.
- Spoon into individual ramekins. Dust with Parmesan cheese, bread crumbs and little dots of remaining butter.
- Brown lightly under the broiler.
- You may make a little thicker by adding more mushrooms.
- You may also serve from a chafing dish with toasted bread rounds.

Serves 6

Shrimp Galliano

peel from 1 large orange	¼ cup Galliano
6 tablespoons clarified butter	¼ cup whipping cream,
12 large, peeled and deveined	beaten to soft peaks
shrimp	watercress
salt and freshly ground	Orange Hollandaise Sauce
pepper	

- Blanch orange peel in boiling water for 2 minutes. Drain.
- Heat butter in heavy large skillet over medium-high heat.
- Add shrimp, salt and pepper and stir until opaque, about 3 minutes.
- Add Galliano.
- Remove from heat and ignite with match. When flames subside, transfer shrimp to plates and keep warm in oven while reducing liquid.
- Boil, cooking liquid until reduced to ¼ cup, about 3 minutes.
- Pour over shrimp.
- Top shrimp with 2 teaspoons of whipped cream.
- Garnish with orange peel, cut into small strips, and watercress and serve with Orange Hollandaise Sauce.

Serves 2

Orange Hollandaise Sauce

2 egg yolks	4½ teaspoons fresh orange
1 tablespoon fresh lemon	juice
juice	salt to taste
½ cup cooled, melted butter	pinch cayenne pepper

- Whisk yolks and lemon juice together in double boiler over barely simmering water until mixture begins to thicken, about 2 minutes.
- Whisk in butter 1 drop at a time.
- Continue whisking until sauce thickens to consistency of whipped cream.
- Whisk in orange juice.
- Season with salt and cayenne pepper.
- Place sauce in serving bowl.

Yields ½ cup

Dr. Bob's Famous Shrimp and Broccoli Casserole

2	heads broccoli, florets only	6	ounces grated mozzarella cheese
2	(10¾-ounce) cans cream of shrimp soup	1½	pounds peeled and deveined shrimp
1	(8-ounce) carton sour cream	½	cup bread crumbs

- Preheat oven to 350 degrees.
- Grease a 9x13-inch dish.
- Arrange broccoli in bottom of dish.
- In separate bowl, mix soup, sour cream and cheese.
- Pour mixture evenly over broccoli.
- Arrange shrimp on top of mixture.
- Bake, uncovered, for 30 minutes.
- Spread bread crumbs evenly over top.
- Bake 5 minutes more.
- Let cool 10 minutes before serving.

Serves 6-8

Creamy Shrimp

1	(8-ounce) package sliced mushrooms		salt and pepper to taste
1	large chopped onion	2	pounds peeled shrimp
1	chopped green pepper	1	(16-ounce) carton sour cream
4	tablespoons butter	2	tablespoons flour
2	chicken bouillon cubes	2	cups cooked, white rice
¼	teaspoon cayenne pepper		

- Sauté mushrooms, onions and peppers in butter in heavy saucepan.
- Add bouillon cubes, cayenne pepper, salt and pepper.
- Add shrimp. Stir until shrimp are pink.
- Stir in sour cream until it bubbles.
- Add flour to thicken.
- Serve over rice.

Serves 6

Shrimp Adlai Stevenson

1 can artichoke hearts	4½ tablespoons flour
¼ cup dry sherry	1½ cups half-and-half
¼ pound sliced mushrooms	salt and pepper to taste
2 tablespoons butter or margarine	1 tablespoon Worcestershire sauce
1 pound peeled and deveined shrimp	¼ cup grated Parmesan cheese
4½ tablespoons butter or margarine	paprika
	chopped parsley (optional)

- Preheat oven to 375 degrees.
- Drain artichoke hearts well. Cut in half and arrange in bottom of a 9x13-inch baking dish.
- Spoon sherry over artichokes.
- Sauté mushrooms in butter. Add to baking dish.
- Place shrimp on top of mushrooms.
- Combine butter, flour, half-and-half, salt, pepper and Worcestershire sauce over medium heat until thick to make cream sauce.
- Pour cream sauce over items in baking dish.
- Sprinkle with Parmesan cheese and dust with paprika.
- Bake for 20 minutes.
- Garnish with parsley if desired.

Serves 8-10

American Frontenac Sardine Fork by Whiting

Grace's Broiled Shrimp

2 cloves finely chopped garlic	3 tablespoons chopped parsley
½ cup oil	2 pounds shelled and
¼ cup soy sauce	deveined shrimp (leave
1 tablespoon lemon juice	tails on)
	8 pieces toasted French bread

- Combine garlic, oil, soy sauce, lemon juice and parsley.
- Arrange shrimp in a 9x13-inch pan.
- Pour liquid over shrimp.
- Marinate shrimp 2 hours.
- Set oven to broil.
- Broil in sauce 7-8 minutes.
- Serve over toasted French bread rounds.

Serves 4

Shrimp in Lemon Butter

1 cup butter or margarine	½ teaspoon black pepper
¼ cup lemon juice	¼ teaspoon salt
1 clove minced garlic	¼ teaspoon garlic powder
1 teaspoon parsley flakes	2 pounds peeled and
1 teaspoon Worcestershire sauce	deveined shrimp
1 teaspoon soy sauce	2 cups cooked, white rice lemon wedges for garnish

- Melt butter in large skillet.
- Add lemon juice, garlic, parsley, Worcestershire sauce, soy sauce, pepper, salt and garlic powder. Bring to a boil.
- Add shrimp. Cook over medium heat 5 minutes, stirring occasionally.
- Serve over fluffy rice.
- Garnish shrimp with lemon wedges.

Serves 4-6

Shrimp with Angel Hair Pasta

4 pounds shrimp (reserve
    heads and peels)
½ bunch chopped scallions
½ cup Sauterne wine
1 tablespoon dried basil
½ cup butter

1½ cups heavy cream
    angel hair pasta, cooked
    according to package
    instructions
½ cup Asiago cheese

- Sauté shrimp-heads and peels, scallions, wine and basil in butter for 3 minutes in heavy saucepan.
- Add cream and cook 3-4 minutes.
- Pour through a strainer, reserving liquid.
- Return to saucepan. Add raw shrimp.
- Cook 4 minutes.
- Pour over pasta.
- Sprinkle cheese over shrimp.

Serves 8

Grilled Shrimp in Foil

1½ pounds large, peeled and
    deveined shrimp
1 (4-ounce) can sliced
    mushrooms, drained
⅓ cup melted butter
2 tablespoons chopped
    scallions

1 tablespoon chili sauce
⅓ cup chopped parsley
¼ teaspoon salt
¼ teaspoon garlic salt
2-3 drops hot pepper sauce
2-3 drops Worcestershire sauce

- Divide shrimp on 2-3 pieces of 10-inch-square aluminum foil.
- Top shrimp with mushrooms.
- Turn up edges of foil on all sides.
- Combine butter, scallions, chili sauce, parsley, salt, garlic salt, hot pepper sauce and Worcestershire sauce.
- Pour over shrimp.
- Double fold edges of foil to make tightly sealed packets.
- Grill on or close to hot coals 5-10 minutes or until done.

Serves 4

Shrimp-Crab Imperial

1 (6-ounce) can crabmeat
1 cup raw rice
1 pound cooked and peeled
   shrimp
½ cup chopped green bell
   pepper
½ cup chopped onion
2 chopped pimentos

1 tablespoon Worcestershire
   sauce
⅛ teaspoon pepper
1 cup chopped celery
1 (4-ounce) can sliced
   mushrooms
¾ cup half-and-half
½ teaspoon salt
1 cup mayonnaise

- Preheat oven to 375 degrees.
- Drain and flake crabmeat.
- Cook rice according to package directions and drain.
- Combine crabmeat, shrimp, bell pepper, onion, pimentos, Worcestershire sauce, pepper, celery, mushrooms, half-and-half, salt and mayonnaise.
- Add to drained rice. Mix until well blended.
- Pour into a 9x13-inch, lightly greased casserole dish.
- Bake covered for 45 minutes.
- Uncover and bake for an additional 15 minutes.

Serves 6-8

Steaming Seafood

Shellfish are done when the shells open or the color changes: pink for shrimp and red for crabs, crayfish and lobster.

clams	5-10 minutes
crab	5-10 minutes
crayfish	5-8 minutes
lobster	5-10 minutes
mussels	4-8 minutes
oysters	8-10 minutes
shrimp	3-5 minutes

Shrimp Creole

2 medium, peeled and chopped tomatoes
3/4 cup chopped onion
3 cloves minced garlic
1/4 cup melted butter or margarine
1/4 cup + 2 tablespoons water
1 (8-ounce) can tomato sauce
1 (6-ounce) can tomato paste

1 1/2 teaspoons chicken-flavored bouillon granules
3/4 teaspoon coarsely ground pepper
3/4 teaspoon dried oregano
3/4 teaspoon dried basil
1/4 teaspoon red pepper
1/8 teaspoon hot pepper sauce
1 1/2 pounds peeled, fresh shrimp

• In a large skillet, sauté tomatoes, onion and garlic in butter.
• Stir in water, tomato sauce, tomato paste, bouillon granules, pepper, oregano, basil, red pepper and hot pepper sauce. Bring to a boil. Mixture will be thick.
• Add shrimp and cover. Reduce heat and simmer over medium heat for 5 minutes until shrimp is done.
• Serve over rice.

Serves 6

Seafood Pasta

4 ounces olive oil
4 ounces white wine
2 dashes soy sauce
   dash of hot pepper sauce (optional)
8 cloves minced garlic
16 ounces heavy cream

1 1/2 pounds peeled and deveined shrimp
1 pound cooked fettuccine
   salt and pepper to taste
4 chopped scallions (optional)
   freshly grated Parmesan cheese

• Combine olive oil, wine, soy sauce, hot pepper sauce, garlic and cream in Dutch oven. Bring to a boil.
• Add shrimp and pasta.
• Cook over low heat about 10 minutes or until shrimp is pink.
• Add salt, pepper and scallions.
• Garnish with Parmesan cheese.

Serves 6-8

Land and Sea Pasta

¼ cup butter, divided
4 cloves minced garlic
1 large can drained
   mushrooms
1 (8-ounce) can undrained,
   minced clams
1 (5½-ounce) can drained
   snow crabmeat

1 pound cleaned and shelled,
   fresh shrimp
1 pound linguini or angel
   hair pasta
¼ cup minced, fresh parsley
4-6 seeded and chopped plum
   tomatoes

- Over medium heat melt 2 tablespoons of butter.
- Add garlic and sauté until garlic is golden.
- Add mushrooms, clams and clam juice, crabmeat and shrimp.
- Heat until sauce begins to thicken and seafood is cooked.
- Boil pasta in salted water until almost al dente and drain. Rinse with cold water to stop cooking.
- In a large skillet, melt remaining 2 tablespoons of butter.
- Add ½ of pasta, ½ of pasta sauce, ½ of parsley and ½ of tomatoes.
- Cook, stirring occasionally, until thoroughly heated.
- Repeat until all portions are heated.
- Variation: Add 1 small can of tomato paste and 1 small can of tomato sauce to seafood mixture as it cools down.

Serves 6

Cooking Times for Fish

For all methods of cooking, these are good rules to follow:
- Measure the fish at the thickest point, and cook fresh fish 10 minutes per inch if cooked alone and 15 minutes per inch if cooked in a sauce.
- Simmer frozen fish 6-9 minutes per ½-inch of thickness.
- Time a poached fish from the moment the liquid starts bubbling again, and begin testing early.

Seafood Newburg

4	tablespoons butter or margarine	½	teaspoon paprika
4	cups raw shrimp, cut in 1-inch pieces	⅛	teaspoon cayenne pepper
		2	cups half-and-half, divided
3	tablespoons lemon juice	3	egg yolks
1	tablespoon flour	2	tablespoons sherry
1	teaspoon salt	1	pound hot, cooked pasta
			parsley for garnish

- In a large frying pan, melt the butter and sauté shrimp for about 5 minutes, stirring constantly.
- Sprinkle with lemon juice.
- Mix the flour, salt, paprika and pepper.
- Add to the seafood and remove from the heat.
- Gradually stir in 1½ cups of half-and-half. Return to the heat until the sauce comes to a simmer.
- Combine the egg yolks with the remaining cream. Blend in ¼ of hot mixture with this.
- Return this to the pan and stir until slightly thickened.
- Add the sherry.
- Serve over pasta and garnish with parsley.

Serves 6-8

Oven-Fried Snapper

¼	cup vegetable oil	½	cup freshly grated Parmesan cheese
1	teaspoon sea salt		
2	cloves crushed garlic	2	pounds fresh snapper fillets
½	cup Italian-seasoned bread crumbs		

- Preheat oven to 500 degrees.
- Combine oil, salt and garlic in a large bowl and set aside.
- Combine bread crumbs and Parmesan cheese.
- Dredge each fillet in oil mixture and then in bread crumb mixture.
- Place fillets in a lightly greased 15x10x1-inch baking pan.
- Bake for 12-15 minutes or until fish flakes easily when tested with a fork.

Serves 6

Shrimp and Florentine Noodle Casserole

1	(8-ounce) box spinach green noodles	1	cup sour cream
2	pounds cleaned shrimp	1	cup mayonnaise
¼	cup butter	1	teaspoon sherry (optional)
1	teaspoon garlic salt	1	tablespoon Dijon mustard
1	can cream of mushroom soup	1	cup grated mozzarella cheese

- Preheat oven to 375 degrees.
- Cook spinach noodles according to package directions.
- Sauté shrimp in butter and garlic salt.
- Mix together mushroom soup, sour cream, mayonnaise, sherry and mustard.
- Add shrimp mixture.
- In a casserole dish, layer ½ of noodles and cover with ½ of shrimp mixture.
- Repeat.
- Cook for 20 minutes.
- Cover with grated mozzarella cheese and bake for another 15 minutes.

Serves 6

Salmon Soufflé

1	(10¾-ounce) can cream of celery soup	1	(7¾-ounce) can of salmon
½	cup grated Cheddar cheese	⅛	teaspoon dill
		6	separated eggs

- Preheat oven to 300 degrees.
- Combine the soup and cheese in a medium saucepan. Heat until cheese melts.
- Drain and debone salmon.
- Stir salmon and dill into soup mixture.
- Beat egg yolks well. Add to mixture.
- Beat egg whites until stiff and fold this lightly into the salmon mixture until blended.
- Bake in an ungreased 2-quart casserole for 1 hour.

Serves 4

Lisa's Linguini with Shrimp and Peppers

1	pound shrimp, heads off and peeled	½	cup dry white wine
3	tablespoons olive oil, divided	½	cup shrimp stock or bottled clam juice
2	cloves chopped garlic	12	ounces linguini
1	medium, chopped onion	4	ounces crumbled Feta cheese
1	red bell pepper, cut in 1-inch strips	¼-½	cup chopped, fresh Italian flat-leaf parsley
1	small green pepper, cut in ½-inch strips	3	tablespoons freshly grated Parmesan cheese
2	tablespoons chopped, fresh oregano or 1 tablespoon dried oregano	¼	teaspoon freshly ground pepper

- In a large skillet, sauté shrimp in 2 tablespoons of the olive oil until just done. Do not overcook.
- Remove shrimp and add 1 tablespoon of olive oil to skillet and sauté garlic, onions, peppers and oregano until softened. Remove mixture from skillet.
- In the same skillet, bring wine and stock to a boil and cook, stirring, until liquid is reduced by ½.
- Add shrimp and onion-pepper mixture to the skillet.
- Cook linguini in salted water until al dente. Drain and rinse with cold water to stop cooking.
- Heat shrimp and pepper mixture well.
- Add hot linguini, Feta cheese, parsley, Parmesan cheese and fresh pepper.
- Mix well and serve.

Serves 6

Tortellini and Shrimp

1 pound medium shrimp	½ teaspoon salt
3 cups fresh cheese tortellini	½ teaspoon pepper
¼ cup butter	¾ cup sour cream
3 tablespoons lemon juice	½ cup plain yogurt
2 cloves minced garlic	6 sliced scallions
4-5 tablespoons dry white wine	½ cup freshly grated
1 teaspoon dried oregano	Parmesan

- Preheat oven to 350 degrees.
- Shell and devein shrimp.
- Cook tortellini according to package directions.
- In a large skillet, melt butter and add lemon juice and garlic. Cook for 2 minutes.
- Add shrimp and sauté for 3-5 minutes.
- Mix together white wine, oregano, salt, pepper, sour cream and yogurt in a large bowl.
- Stir shrimp mixture into cream mixture.
- Pour into a 2-quart casserole.
- Top with scallions and Parmesan cheese.
- Bake for 20 minutes.

Serves 6-8

Lamb with Green Pepper and Carrots

1 cup julienned carrots	1 medium, julienned green pepper
2 tablespoons olive oil	½ teaspoon ground coriander
2 cloves chopped garlic	salt
¾ pound boneless lamb, trimmed of fat and julienned	white pepper

- Steam carrots.
- Heat skillet with oil and garlic.
- Add lamb and stir-fry until browned.
- Add steamed carrots and green pepper to skillet.
- Stir until hot and tender.
- Add coriander, salt and pepper.

Serves 4-6

Grilled, Marinated Leg of Lamb

1 boned leg of lamb
1 cup extra-virgin olive oil
⅓ cup balsamic vinegar
½ cup chopped, fresh cilantro
  leaves

2 tablespoons crushed black
  peppercorns
4 cloves crushed garlic

- Have butcher bone lamb.
- Pound meat to equal thickness for even grilling. If meat is unmanageable, cut into 2 pieces.
- Mix olive oil, vinegar, cilantro, peppercorns and garlic for marinade.
- Place meat in zippered plastic bag or deep non-metal bowl and pour marinade over meat.
- Prepare the day before and store meat in refrigerator, turning meat in marinade several times.
- Grill 30-40 minutes for rare, depending on thickness of meat.
- Slice thin to serve.

Serves 8-10

Herb-Roasted Rack of Lamb

¼ teaspoon ground thyme
¼ teaspoon black pepper
⅛ teaspoon onion powder
¼ teaspoon monosodium
  glutamate (optional)

½ teaspoon seasoning salt
½ teaspoon salt
1 (8-rib) rack of lamb
  (about 2½ pounds)

- Preheat oven to 325 degrees.
- Combine thyme, black pepper, onion powder, monosodium glutamate and salts.
- Rub seasonings on lamb.
- Place lamb on rack in a shallow pan, fat side up.
- Bake for 30 minutes per pound to desired degree of doneness.
- Serve hot.
- Excellent with mint jelly.

Serves 4

Soft Shell Crab à la Toulouse

5-6 soft shell crab or grouper
½ teaspoon lemon dill
½ teaspoon herbes de Provence
⅛ teaspoon salt
⅛ teaspoon pepper
¼ cup flour to dust crabs

⅛ cup olive oil
2 tablespoons capers
1 small can sliced black olives
juice of 1 small lemon
½-¾ cup marsala wine

- Season crab with lemon dill, herbes de Provence, salt and pepper.
- Dust crabs lightly with flour.
- Sauté in oil 6-7 minutes on each side, only turning once during cooking.
- Place on a platter to keep warm.
- Scrape the scrapings from the pan and add to them the capers, olives, lemon juice and wine.
- Reduce sauce by ½ and serve over crabs.
- When substituting grouper for crab, cook the grouper for 10 minutes on each side.

Serves 5

Vidalia Onion Tart

¼ cup butter
1 cup crushed saltines
2 thinly sliced Vidalia onions
2 tablespoons butter
¾ cup milk

2 eggs
¾ teaspoon salt
pepper to taste
¼ cup grated Cheddar cheese
paprika

- Preheat oven to 350 degrees.
- Melt ¼ cup butter and mix with crackers.
- Press into 9-inch pie plate or tart pan.
- Sauté onions until tender in 2 tablespoons butter.
- Place onions in cracker crumb shell.
- Combine milk, eggs, salt and pepper and pour over onions.
- Sprinkle with cheese and paprika.
- Bake for 20-30 minutes.

Serves 6

Spinach Lasagna

1	(16-ounce) carton ricotta cheese or small-curd cottage cheese	1	teaspoon salt
1½	cups shredded mozzarella cheese, divided	½	teaspoon pepper
1	egg	¾	teaspoon oregano
2	(10-ounce) packages frozen spinach, thawed and drained	2	(15½-ounce) jars spaghetti sauce
		1	(8-ounce) package uncooked lasagna noodles
		1	cup water

- Preheat oven to 350 degrees.
- In a large bowl, combine ricotta, 1 cup mozzarella cheese, egg, spinach, salt, pepper and oregano.
- Spread ½ cup spaghetti sauce in greased 13x9-inch pan.
- Place ⅓ of noodles over sauce and cover with ½ of cheese mixture.
- Repeat layers.
- Top with remaining noodles, spaghetti sauce and mozzarella cheese.
- Pour water around edges and cover tightly with foil.
- Bake for 1 hour and 15 minutes.
- Let stand 15 minutes before serving.

Serves 8-12

Homegrown Tomato Pie

1	(8-inch) pie crust	3-4 chopped scallions
2	medium, sliced tomatoes	1 cup mayonnaise
1	pound cooked and crumbled bacon	1 cup grated Cheddar or American cheese

- Preheat oven to 350 degrees.
- Place tomatoes on bottom of pie crust.
- Spread crumbled bacon and scallions on tomatoes.
- Mix mayonnaise and cheese together and spread on top of pie.
- Bake for 30 minutes.

Serves 6

Sausage Bread

3-4 loaves frozen bread dough	1 chopped onion
1 pound hot sausage	1 cup grated Cheddar cheese
1 pound mild sausage	1 cup grated mozzarella
1 chopped bell pepper	cheese

- Thaw bread dough according to package directions.
- Preheat oven to 375 degrees.
- Brown sausage, bell pepper and onion. Drain well.
- Spray foil with cooking spray.
- Roll out loaves of dough onto the foil to ¼-inch thickness.
- Place sausage mixture in the center of the dough. Top with cheeses.
- Fold dough together to enclose sausage filling.
- Place seam side down and bake uncovered for 25-30 minutes or until top is golden brown.
- To serve, slice while hot.

Serves 18-20

Tomato Sauce for Pasta

2 teaspoons olive oil	2 teaspoons lemon juice
6 cloves of crushed garlic	1 teaspoon sugar
1 small, minced onion	¼ cup red wine
1 (28-ounce) can crushed tomatoes	¼ teaspoon salt
	pasta of your choice
1 (8-ounce) can tomato sauce	¼ cup freshly grated
1 (6-ounce) can tomato paste	Parmesan cheese
1 small fresh jalapeño	

- Heat oil, add garlic and onion. Sauté until tender.
- Add tomatoes, tomato sauce and tomato paste.
- Cut fresh jalapeño into thirds and add to tomato mixture.
- Simmer for 30 minutes.
- Remove jalapeño.
- Add lemon juice, sugar, red wine and salt.
- Serve over cooked pasta.
- Top with Parmesan cheese.

Serves 8

Walnut Sauce for Pasta

3 cloves minced garlic	1 cup walnuts, broken into
1 cup thinly sliced onion	small pieces
½ cup olive oil	4 tablespoons fresh parsley
¼ teaspoon dried red pepper	½ cup dry white wine
flakes	1 pound cooked penne pasta
	4 ounces Feta cheese

- In a skillet, sauté garlic and onion in olive oil. Cook onion until it is transparent.
- Add red pepper flakes, walnuts and 3 tablespoons of the parsley. Sauté briefly.
- Add the white wine and cook for 2 minutes.
- Cover and keep warm.
- Prepare pasta in salted water.
- Drain and place in a warm pasta bowl.
- Pour warm walnut sauce over pasta and toss.
- Top with Feta cheese and remaining parsley.
- Toss again lightly and serve at once.

Serves 8

Carolyn's Homemade Mayonnaise

juice of 1 large lime or lemon	1-2 tablespoons crushed red pepper
1 teaspoon sugar	1 egg
1 teaspoon dry mustard	2 cups vegetable oil or
salt to taste	1½ cups vegetable and
	½ cup sesame oil

- In a mixing bowl, mix juice, sugar, mustard, salt and pepper.
- In blender or processor beat egg until frothy.
- Slowly add oil, processing the entire time.
- When smooth, slowly add juice mixture.
- Refrigerate.

Yields 2 cups

Town and Country Omelet

3	tablespoons canola oil	8	medium eggs
1	tablespoon unsalted butter	½	cup coarsely chopped
2	medium, white onions, peeled and thinly sliced		chives
		¾	teaspoon salt
1¼	pounds potatoes, peeled and thinly sliced	½	teaspoon freshly ground pepper
1	large, sliced tomato		

- Heat oil and butter in non-stick skillet until hot, but not smoky.
- Add onions and potatoes. Cook covered for 15-20 minutes on low heat, stirring occasionally.
- Arrange sliced tomatoes to cover most of surface of the mixture. Cover and cook 1 minute.
- Combine eggs, chives, salt and pepper. Blend until smooth.
- Add egg mixture to skillet, stirring gently with tines of fork to allow egg to flow between potatoes.
- Preheat oven to broil.
- Place skillet 3-4 inches under hot broiler.
- Cook 3 minutes until eggs are set.
- Invert onto a platter.
- Cut into wedges and serve.

Serves 6

Pork Tenderloin Marinade

½	cup soy sauce	4	minced cloves garlic
3	tablespoons Worcestershire sauce	3	tablespoons brown sugar
		1	tablespoon peanut oil

- Combine soy sauce, Worcestershire sauce, garlic, brown sugar and peanut oil.
- Marinate pork tenderloin a minimum of 2 hours and as long as overnight.

Yields ¾ cup

Secret Sweet and Hot Special Mustard

2 cups sugar	¼ teaspoon black pepper
1½ cups cider vinegar	¼ teaspoon white pepper
1 teaspoon salt	⅓-½ cup water
1½ cups dry mustard	3 eggs
⅛ teaspoon red pepper	½ cup butter

• In a large saucepan, mix sugar, vinegar and salt. Boil until sugar dissolves.
• In a glass mixing bowl, cream dry mustard, peppers and water into a thick paste.
• In a blender or processor scrape paste in bowl and slowly add vinegar mixture. Drizzle into paste until all is incorporated.
• Pour back into saucepan and return to stove.
• On low heat, bring to a boil, stirring constantly. Remove from heat.
• In a small bowl, beat eggs very well and add a small amount of hot mixture, to temper. Add egg mixture to saucepan and return to stove.
• Slowly boil for a few minutes, stirring constantly.
• Remove from heat and add butter. Cool.
• Pour into 5 (8-ounce) jars and refrigerate.
• Excellent for a dip or sandwich spread or with crackers.

Yields 5 (8-ounce) jars

This sauce was enjoyed by many, but the cook refused to share the recipe with even her closest friends. One night several of them kept her occupied, while the others went to her home and searched for and stole her wonderful recipe. Little does she know that today we are benefiting from their creative recipe search.

Beef Tenderloin Marinade

½ cup teriyaki sauce	½ cup Italian dressing
½ cup Worcestershire sauce	

• Combine teriyaki sauce, Worcestershire sauce and dressing.
• Marinate beef tenderloin for 3-5 hours.

Yields 1½ cups

Sauce for Cold Chicken

2 teaspoons Dijon mustard	½ teaspoon salt
2 tablespoons balsamic vinegar	½ teaspoon pepper
	3 tablespoons olive oil

• Combine mustard, vinegar, salt, pepper and olive oil.
• Chill and allow flavors to blend.
• Serve with cold baked, grilled or broiled chicken.

Yields ½ cup

Mustard Sauce for Seafood

¼ cup Dijon mustard	¼ cup white wine vinegar
½ teaspoon artificial sweetener	¼ cup plain yogurt
	¼ cup chopped dill

• Combine mustard, sweetener, vinegar, yogurt and dill.
• Chill. Will keep 2-3 weeks in refrigerator.

Yields 1 cup

Grandmother's Tartar Sauce

1 cup homemade mayonnaise	½ tablespoon finely chopped olives
2 tablespoons capers	½ tablespoon finely chopped parsley
½ tablespoon finely chopped dill pickle	

• Mix mayonnaise, capers, pickle, olives and parsley.
• Chill to blend flavors.

Yields 1 cup

Newport Scroll

Side Dishes

Newport Scroll

Side Dishes

Newport Scroll
Gorham Corporation
Providence, Rhode Island

Newport Scroll, introduced in 1989, is a reinterpretation of an English design which first appeared around the middle of the 18th Century. In the past, the basic style has been called sometimes Onslow and sometimes Scroll. In the contemporary version (designer unknown), linear decoration runs the length of the flaring stem and curves around the backward-scrolling terminal. Newport Scroll is a popular pattern.

For a history of the Gorham Corporation, see discussion under Strasbourg.

Pictured: English, covered entrée dish; Newport Scroll place setting; Versaille serving spoon and English serving spoon, patented 1891

Asparagus with Basil-Mayonnaise Sauce

2   pounds fresh asparagus or
        2 (10-ounce) frozen
        packages
1   cup mayonnaise
1   tablespoon lemon juice

1   teaspoon basil
¼   teaspoon pepper
1   medium, peeled and
        finely chopped tomato

- Wash and trim asparagus. Cook asparagus (make sure not to overcook) and drain.
- Combine mayonnaise, lemon juice, basil and pepper.
- Heat slowly, stirring constantly, until very warm.
- Remove from heat and stir in tomatoes.
- Place asparagus spears on plate and spoon sauce over them.

Serves 6

Green Beans with Horseradish Sauce

7   slices bacon
2   (9-ounce) packages frozen
        Italian-style green beans,
        thawed
6   medium, thinly sliced
        carrots

2   tablespoons butter
2   cloves minced garlic
½   teaspoon pepper
½   cup mayonnaise
½   cup sour cream
⅓   cup horseradish

- Cook bacon until crisp. Reserve 2 tablespoons of bacon drippings.
- Add green beans, carrots, butter, garlic and pepper to skillet.
- In bacon grease, stir-fry over medium-high about 5 minutes, or until tender and crisp.
- Crumble bacon and stir into beans.
- To make sauce, combine mayonnaise, sour cream and horseradish and mix well.
- Serve beans with horseradish sauce.

Serves 8

Savory Green Beans

3 (16-ounce) cans green beans or 2 pounds fresh, clean and cut
¼ teaspoon nutmeg
3 cups chicken broth
2 tablespoons bacon grease

2 tablespoons flour
1 tablespoon white vinegar
¼ cup chopped onion
½ teaspoon dried savory
1 teaspoon minced parsley
½ teaspoon sugar

- Put beans into large saucepan with nutmeg, broth and bacon grease. Simmer until beans are cooked, about 20 minutes.
- Blend flour into vinegar; add to beans along with onion, savory, parsley and sugar.
- Simmer 30 minutes to 1 hour to blend flavors.

Serves 8

Swiss-Style Green Beans

2 tablespoons butter, divided
2 tablespoons flour
½ teaspoon sugar
½ teaspoon salt
⅛ teaspoon pepper

¼ teaspoon grated onion
½ cup sour cream
2 cups drained green beans
¼ pound grated Swiss cheese
1 cup cornflakes

- Preheat oven to 400 degrees.
- Melt 1 tablespoon butter; stir in flour, sugar, salt, pepper and onion.
- Add sour cream gradually, stirring constantly. Cook until thick.
- Fold in green beans.
- Pour mixture into greased casserole.
- Sprinkle with grated Swiss cheese.
- Crush cornflakes into fine crumbs and mix with remaining melted butter. Sprinkle over beans.
- Bake for 20 minutes, uncovered.

Serves 4

Broccoli with Parmesan Sauce

1 pound fresh broccoli
   vegetable cooking spray
¼ cup chopped, sweet red
   pepper
¼ cup chopped onion
2 teaspoons reduced-calorie
   margarine

1 teaspoon flour
½ cup skim milk
1 ounce fat-free cream cheese
3 tablespoons freshly grated
   Parmesan cheese
¼ teaspoon garlic powder

- Cut broccoli into spears.
- Cook until tender and crisp; transfer to serving platter and keep warm.
- Coat heavy saucepan with spray. Place saucepan over medium-high until hot.
- Add pepper and onion. Sauté 3-4 minutes until tender.
- Remove pepper and onion from pan and set aside.
- Melt margarine in pan over medium heat.
- Add flour and stir until smooth. Cook 1 minute, stirring constantly.
- Add milk gradually and cook, stirring constantly, until slightly thickened.
- Add sautéed peppers and onions, cream cheese, Parmesan cheese and garlic powder.
- Cook over low heat until cheese melts.
- Spoon over broccoli and serve.

Serves 6

Broccoli with Zesty Sauce

1 large bunch fresh broccoli
   or 2 packages frozen
   broccoli
2 tablespoons butter
2 tablespoons minced onion
1½ cups sour cream

2 teaspoons sugar
1 teaspoon vinegar
½ teaspoon poppy seed
½ teaspoon paprika
¼ teaspoon salt
   pepper

- Cook broccoli until tender and drain well.
- Melt butter and add onion and sauté.
- Remove from heat and stir in sour cream, sugar, vinegar, poppy seed, paprika, salt and pepper.
- Arrange broccoli on heated platter and cover with sour cream zesty sauce.

Serves 4-6

Carrots Vicky

2 tablespoons minced, yellow
   onion
4 tablespoons butter or
   margarine
8 carrots, peeled and
   thinly sliced

¼ teaspoon salt
2 tablespoons sugar
½ cup water
1 tablespoon minced, fresh
   parsley

- Sauté onion in butter until transparent.
- Add carrots, salt, sugar and water.
- Cover and cook on medium heat for 8-10 minutes.
- Serve garnished with parsley.

Serves 4

Baked, Honey-Glazed Carrots

½ cup dark brown sugar
1½ teaspoons cornstarch
¼ teaspoon salt
1 cup water
1 small can crushed
   pineapple, drained
   (reserve liquid)

2 tablespoons butter or
   margarine
1 tablespoon honey
1 (16-ounce) package cooked
   baby carrots

- Preheat oven to 350 degrees.
- Blend sugar, cornstarch and salt in small saucepan.
- Add 1 cup water and reserved pineapple juice.
- Cook 7-8 minutes until thin syrup consistency.
- Remove from heat and add 2 tablespoons butter and 1 tablespoon honey.
- Put cooked carrots and pineapple in casserole dish and cover with syrup mixture.
- Bake for 30-40 minutes.

Serves 8

Eggplant Casserole

1 eggplant, approximately 1¼ pounds cooking oil	1 clove minced garlic
6-8 slices bacon	1 pound fresh or canned tomatoes, cut in chunks
1 medium, chopped onion	2 tablespoons brown sugar
1 chopped green pepper	salt and pepper to taste
½ pound sliced mushrooms	2 cups shredded mozzarella cheese

- Preheat oven to 450 degrees.
- Peel eggplant and cut into ½-inch slices. Brush both sides with oil.
- Bake for 20 minutes on uncovered baking sheet.
- Reduce oven heat to 350 degrees.
- Fry bacon until crisp. Drain bacon and crumble. Reserve 2 tablespoons of drippings.
- Add onion, green pepper, mushrooms and garlic to drippings.
- Sauté until limp.
- Stir in tomatoes and their liquid, sugar, salt and pepper.
- Cook over medium-high heat, uncovered, until most of the liquid has evaporated.
- Layer eggplant, bacon and sauce in shallow, 2-quart casserole.
- Top with cheese and bake, uncovered, until bubbly, about 15 minutes.

Serves 6

Darlene's Corn Pudding

⅔ cup vegetable oil	4 beaten eggs
1 package Mexican cornbread mix	4-6 ounces grated Cheddar cheese
2 cans cream-style corn	1 small chopped onion

- Preheat oven to 350 degrees.
- Mix oil, cornbread mix, corn, eggs, cheese and onion together.
- Bake for 30 minutes until set.

Serves 8-10

Virginia Eggplant

1 large, peeled and sliced eggplant	1 cup grated Cheddar cheese
salt to taste	1 cup peeled and deveined, small shrimp
pepper to taste	1 tablespoon flour
1 large, chopped onion	1 teaspoon seasoning salt
1 large, chopped green pepper	1 teaspoon pepper
4 tablespoons butter	1 tablespoon half-and-half
1 cup chopped oysters with juice	¼ teaspoon celery seeds
	buttered bread crumbs

- Preheat oven to 350 degrees.
- Parboil eggplant until tender. Drain well and add salt and pepper.
- Sauté onion and green pepper in butter until tender.
- Combine onion, green pepper, oysters, cheese, shrimp, flour and seasoning salt.
- Add 1 tablespoon of half-and-half to make creamy (more if needed).
- Place eggplant in bottom of 3-quart, greased casserole dish. Top with cream mixture. Add celery seeds and bread crumbs.
- Bake for 45 minutes.

Serves 6-8

Garlic Mashed Potatoes

4 pounds potatoes	1 cup canned, low-salt chicken broth, warmed
8 cloves peeled and crushed garlic	½ cup grated Parmesan cheese
2 tablespoons butter	salt and pepper to taste
2 tablespoons fresh, chopped rosemary	

- Peel potatoes and cut into 1-inch cubes. Rinse well.
- Cook potatoes and garlic in boiling salted water for 30 minutes or until very tender. Drain.
- In a bowl, beat potatoes and garlic with an electric mixer. Add butter and rosemary.
- Slowly beat warm chicken broth into potatoes until smooth.
- Stir in Parmesan cheese, salt and pepper to taste.

Serves 8

Baked Mushrooms

2	pounds fresh mushrooms	1	teaspoon salt
¼	cup butter or margarine, divided	2	teaspoons lemon juice
1	clove chopped garlic	½	teaspoon sage
½	cup chopped onion	½	cup chopped parsley
¼	cup fresh bread crumbs	¼	cup olive oil
		¼	cup white wine

- Preheat oven to 325 degrees.
- Clean the mushrooms and separate the stems from the caps. Chop the stems.
- Heat ⅛ cup butter in a heavy frying pan. Add garlic, onions and chopped stems. Sauté until the onions are tender.
- Remove from the heat and stir in the bread crumbs, salt, lemon juice, sage and all but 1 tablespoon of the parsley.
- Pour the oil into a baking dish and coat well. Place ½ the mushroom caps, hollow side up, in an even layer on the bottom.
- Cover with the bread crumb mixture and top with the remaining mushroom caps, rounded sides up.
- Dot with the remaining butter and pour the wine over all the mushrooms.
- Bake for 30 minutes, until the mushrooms are brown and tender.
- Garnish with remaining parsley.

Serves 6

Oven-Baked Potatoes

6	medium, unpeeled potatoes	¾	teaspoon salt
3	medium onions	¼	teaspoon pepper
½	cup butter or margarine	¼	teaspoon celery seed
1	crushed garlic clove	¼	teaspoon paprika

- Preheat oven to 400 degrees.
- Cut potatoes and onions into ¼-inch slices. Alternate slices, slightly overlapping, in a single layer in a 13x9x2-inch casserole dish.
- Melt butter and add garlic, salt, pepper, celery seed and paprika.
- Drizzle over potatoes and onion slices.
- Cover and bake for 40 minutes.
- Sprinkle with paprika and bake, uncovered, for 20 minutes.

Serves 8

Lemon-Horseradish New Potatoes

12 tiny, new potatoes (1½ pounds)	1 tablespoon prepared horseradish
4 tablespoons butter	2 teaspoons lemon juice
½ teaspoon salt	1 thinly sliced lemon
¼ teaspoon pepper	2 tablespoons chopped, fresh parsley

- Preheat oven to 350 degrees.
- Wash potatoes and peel a ½-inch strip around the center of each potato.
- In a 2-quart casserole melt butter; add salt, pepper, horseradish and lemon juice.
- Add potatoes and stir until well coated with butter mixture.
- Cover and bake for 55-65 minutes or until potatoes are tender.
- Garnish with lemon and parsley.

Serves 4-6

Marjoram Potatoes

½ cup freshly grated Parmesan cheese	¼ teaspoon nutmeg
2½ teaspoons dried marjoram	¼ teaspoon ground pepper
1 teaspoon salt	3 pounds red potatoes
½ teaspoon garlic powder	1¾ cups whipping cream
	½ cup water

- Preheat oven to 350 degrees.
- Combine cheese, marjoram, salt, garlic powder, nutmeg and pepper. Set aside.
- Thinly slice potatoes. Layer potatoes into a 13x9-inch greased casserole dish.
- Layer with seasoning mixture, then potatoes, then seasoning mixture, ending with potatoes.
- Combine whipping cream and water; pour over potatoes.
- Bake, covered with foil, for 1 hour and 20 minutes.
- Bake an additional 30 minutes, uncovered, until browned.

Serves 8

Perfect Mashed Potatoes

8   medium potatoes
1   small, finely chopped
    onion
½   cup milk
⅓   cup margarine

1   teaspoon freshly grated
    Parmesan cheese
1   teaspoon salt
¼   teaspoon sugar
⅛   teaspoon pepper

- Peel potatoes and slice into cubes.
- Cook potatoes and onion in boiling water for 20 minutes or until tender.
- Drain and mash potatoes and onions.
- Add milk, margarine, cheese, salt, sugar and pepper and mix until smooth.

Serves 8

Potato Medley

5   Russet potatoes
3   peeled yams
2   red onions
2   red peppers

1   medium, peeled butternut
    squash
3   tablespoons olive oil,
    divided
    salt and pepper to taste

- Preheat oven to 400 degrees.
- Cut potatoes, yams, onions, peppers and squash into ½-inch chunks.
- Toss potatoes, yams and squash with 2 tablespoons olive oil, so that all sides are coated.
- Spread vegetables in a single layer in a large shallow baking dish and put in oven for 10 minutes.
- Toss onions and peppers with remaining oil. Add to pan in oven, sprinkle with salt and pepper and roast until vegetables are browned and begin to dehydrate, about another 20 minutes.
- Serve hot or cold.

Serves 8-10

Potatoes au Gratin

1½ pounds potatoes
2   cups heavy cream
2   cups half-and-half
1   large clove puréed garlic
¾   teaspoon salt

pepper to taste
nutmeg to taste
8   ounces grated Monterey
    Jack cheese

- Peel and slice potatoes ⅛-inch thick.
- Place potatoes in large Dutch oven, layering with cream, half-and-half, garlic, salt, pepper and nutmeg between layers.
- Heat to just below simmer and maintain there for 1 hour, or until potatoes are tender. Do not boil freely or cream will curdle.
- Preheat oven to 425 degrees.
- Pour into greased 8½x11-inch oblong casserole.
- Top with cheese.
- Bake for 20 minutes or until bubbly hot and lightly browned.

Serves 4

Rosemary Potatoes

6-8 medium, red-skinned
    potatoes
    salt and pepper

3   tablespoons rosemary
¼   cup olive oil

- Preheat oven to 375 degrees.
- To create a fan, cut potatoes at ⅛-inch intervals across the top, but not all the way through.
- Place on baking sheet.
- Salt and pepper the potatoes.
- Mix rosemary and olive oil together. Drizzle over the top of each potato.
- Bake for 45 minutes.
- Baste with oil mixture every 15 minutes.

Serves 6

Spicy Oven Fries

4 large Idaho potatoes	2 tablespoons butter
¼ cup olive oil	2 tablespoons herbed salt

- Preheat oven to 450 degrees.
- Cut unpeeled potatoes into thick fries, about ¾-inch thick.
- Lay out potatoes on paper towels to dry.
- Mix olive oil and butter. Brush mixture on large baking sheet.
- Arrange potatoes on sheet and brush with butter mixture.
- Bake until light brown, about 20 minutes.
- Sprinkle with herbed salt and bake 10-15 minutes more or until brown and tender.
- Serve at once.

Serves 6-8

Herbed Salt

½ cup Kosher salt	½ teaspoon ground ginger
6 garlic cloves	½ teaspoon dry mustard
2 teaspoons paprika	½ teaspoon celery seed
2 teaspoons chili powder	1 teaspoon dried thyme
1 teaspoon freshly ground white pepper	½ teaspoon dried rosemary

- Put coarse salt in food processor. Turn on and drop in garlic to mince.
- Add paprika, chili powder, pepper, ginger, mustard, celery seed, thyme and dried rosemary; quickly pulse in.
- Store in pantry for use on potatoes, meats or vegetables. Use sparingly.

Yields ¾ cup

Sweet Potato Amaretto

½ cup raisins
½ cup amaretto
2 (29-ounce) cans yams,
   mashed and drained
2 well beaten eggs

½ cup milk
1 cup brown sugar
1 cup chopped pecans
1½ cups small marshmallows

- Soak raisins in warm amaretto for 1 hour.
- Preheat oven to 350 degrees.
- Mix together yams, eggs, milk, brown sugar and pecans.
- Add raisin and amaretto mixture.
- Place in greased 10x10x2-inch casserole dish.
- Bake for 30 minutes.
- Remove from oven and top with marshmallows.
- Bake for 3-5 minutes, until marshmallows are slightly brown and melted.

Serves 8-10

Pineapple Sweet Potato Casserole

½ cup melted butter or
   margarine, divided
2 cups cooked and mashed
   sweet potatoes
¼ cup milk
1 cup sugar
1 teaspoon vanilla

2 eggs
1 small can pineapple,
   drained
¼ cup all-purpose flour
½ cup sugar
1 egg

- Preheat oven to 350 degrees.
- Melt ¼ cup butter.
- Add sweet potatoes, milk, 1 cup sugar, vanilla and eggs. Mix well and pour into casserole dish.
- Drain pineapple and mix with flour, ½ cup sugar, egg and remaining ¼ cup melted butter.
- Pour on top of casserole mixture.
- Bake for 45 minutes.

Serves 6

Orange and Rum Sweet Potatoes

2   pounds sweet potatoes
1   cup packed brown sugar, divided
¼   cup melted butter, divided
½   teaspoon salt

2   tablespoons rum
2   oranges, peeled and segmented
¾   cup chopped nuts

• Preheat oven to 375 degrees.
• Boil sweet potatoes in their skin until tender.
• Drain, cool and peel potatoes.
• Mash potatoes very smooth, then beat in ¼ cup brown sugar, ½ the butter, salt and rum.
• Cut orange segments in half crosswise and remove pits.
• Fold orange segments into sweet potato mixture.
• Pour into a buttered 2-quart casserole.
• Mix together the nuts, remaining brown sugar and butter.
• Sprinkle mixture over top of casserole.
• Bake for 30 minutes.

Serves 6-10

Spinach Supreme

1   (10-ounce) package frozen leaf spinach
2   teaspoons butter
1   tablespoon fresh lemon juice
¼   teaspoon dry mustard

½   cup sliced, fresh mushrooms
¼   cup thinly sliced red onion
    coarsely ground black pepper

• Cook spinach according to package directions.
• Drain well and place on heated platter.
• Melt butter in 1-quart saucepan. Stir in lemon juice and mustard.
• Add mushrooms and onions.
• Sauté until tender.
• Pour over spinach.
• Sprinkle with pepper

Serves 4

Artichoke and Spinach Casserole

2 (10-ounce) packages
     chopped, frozen spinach
3 tablespoons melted butter
2 (3-ounce) packages
     softened cream cheese
     juice of ½ lemon
¼ teaspoon salt

¼ teaspoon pepper
¼ teaspoon nutmeg
1 (14-ounce) can artichoke
     hearts
1 sleeve round, butter-
     flavored crackers,
     crumbled

- Preheat oven to 350 degrees.
- Grease a 2-quart casserole.
- Cook spinach and drain well.
- Add butter, cream cheese, lemon juice, salt, pepper and nutmeg to spinach. Blend.
- Cut artichokes in quarters. Place in bottom of greased casserole.
- Add spinach mixture.
- Top with cracker crumbs and dot with butter.
- Bake for 25 minutes.

Serves 6

Butternut Squash and Apple Bake

2 pounds butternut squash
½ cup packed brown sugar
½ cup melted margarine
1 tablespoon flour

1 teaspoon salt
½ teaspoon mace
2 baking apples, cored and
     sliced ½-inch thick

- Preheat oven to 350 degrees.
- Cut squash in half. Remove seeds and fibers, and pare ½-inch slices.
- Stir brown sugar, margarine, flour, salt and mace together.
- Arrange squash in ungreased baking dish (11½x7½x1½-inch). Top with apples and sprinkle with brown sugar mixture.
- Cover with foil and bake 50-60 minutes.

Serves 5-6

Creamy Spinach Casserole

2 cups bite-sized, crispy rice cereal squares
1 teaspoon onion powder
3 tablespoons melted butter
1 (8-ounce) package cream cheese
1 (5-ounce) can evaporated milk
2 teaspoons lemon juice

¾ teaspoon seasoning salt
dash pepper
1 beaten egg
1 (8-ounce) can sliced mushrooms, reserve ¼ of liquid
2 (10-ounce) packages frozen spinach, cooked and drained

- Preheat oven to 350 degrees.
- Combine cereal, onion powder and butter and set aside.
- In a saucepan, combine cream cheese, milk, lemon juice, seasoning salt, pepper and liquid.
- Cook and stir on low until smooth.
- Add egg; cook and stir constantly until thickened.
- Stir in mushrooms and spinach.
- Pour into 1½-quart casserole.
- Add cereal topping.
- Bake for 15-20 minutes.

Serves 8

Mary's Turnip Greens

1½ pounds turnip greens or big bunch with roots or plain
1 cup water
2 tablespoons honey

2 tablespoons sugar
1 small piece pork
1 teaspoon salt
1 small, chopped onion

- Remove pulpy stems of turnip greens. Wash greens thoroughly in salted water; set aside.
- Combine water, honey, sugar, pork, salt and onion in a large saucepan and bring to a boil.
- Add greens, reduce heat and simmer about an hour or until very tender.
- Serve with cornbread.

Serves 4-6

Chu-Chu's Squash Casserole

8 small, sliced squash	salt to taste
1 medium, sliced onion	white sauce
1 cup grated cheese	

- Preheat oven to 350 degrees.
- Cook squash in boiling water for 5 minutes. Drain and add onion.
- Add white sauce to squash mixture.
- Salt to taste.
- Bake for 20 minutes.
- Sprinkle cheese on top and put back into oven until cheese melts.

Serves 4-6

White Sauce

2 tablespoons flour	1½ cups milk
3 tablespoons butter	salt and pepper to taste

- Blend flour and butter in a saucepan.
- Gradually add milk; add salt and pepper.
- Cook until sauce is of medium thickness.

Yields 1 cup

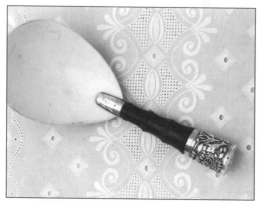

18th Century Serving Spoon with
Shell Bowl and Bone Handle from
Augsburg, Germany

Oven-Roasted Plum Tomatoes

12 plum tomatoes, cored and
   sliced lengthwise into
   ½-inch slices
¼ cup extra-virgin olive oil
2 cloves garlic
1 tablespoon minced shallot

1 teaspoon dried basil
½ teaspoon dried oregano
¼ teaspoon dried thyme
1 teaspoon freshly ground
   black pepper
½ teaspoon salt

- Preheat oven to 250 degrees.
- Toss cored tomatoes, olive oil, garlic, shallots, basil, oregano, thyme, pepper and salt together until the tomato slices are evenly coated.
- Lay the tomato slices on a wire rack and place the rack on a baking sheet to catch the drippings.
- Roast the tomatoes in the warm oven until they have lost most of their moisture and are slightly leathery in appearance, about 2 hours.
- Remove from the oven and leave on the rack to cool.
- Serve at room temperature or chilled.

Serves 10-12

Tomato Casserole

1 large, chopped onion
1 chopped bell pepper
1 teaspoon bacon grease
6 slices dried toast
2 cans chopped tomatoes

6 slices crumbled, crisp
   bacon
½ pound grated New York
   Cheddar cheese
½ cup brown sugar
   salt and pepper

- Preheat oven to 300 degrees.
- Brown onion and bell pepper in bacon grease.
- Crumble dry toast in large oblong dish.
- Combine onion and bell pepper mixture with tomatoes, bacon, cheese, sugar, salt and pepper to taste. Pour over toast crumbs.
- Bake 1 hour.

Serves 10-12

Tomatoes à Quesa

4	medium, thinly sliced onions	1	cup bread crumbs
3	tablespoons butter		salt and pepper to taste
6	large, thinly sliced tomatoes	2	beaten eggs
1½	cups grated, sharp Cheddar cheese	1	cup sour cream
		1	teaspoon paprika

- Preheat oven to 375 degrees.
- In a 10-inch skillet, sauté onions in butter for 5 minutes over medium heat. Set onion mixture aside.
- Grease a 2-quart casserole and arrange a layer of tomatoes on the bottom.
- Sprinkle some of the cheese on top followed by bread crumbs, sautéed onions, salt and pepper.
- Repeat layers until all ingredients are used, ending with cheese. (This makes 3 layers of tomatoes and 2 layers of onions.)
- In a small mixing bowl beat the eggs and sour cream until smooth. Pour sour cream over casserole and sprinkle with paprika.
- Bake covered for 30 minutes, then uncover and bake 15 minutes longer until puffed and lightly browned.

Serves 8

Stuffed Tomatoes

3	cups crumbled cornbread	½	cup chopped mushrooms
½	teaspoon oregano	1	clove crushed garlic
½	teaspoon salt	2	tablespoons melted butter
	dash pepper	6	tomatoes
1	egg		

- Preheat oven to 400 degrees.
- Combine cornbread, oregano, salt, pepper and egg.
- Sauté mushrooms in butter and garlic. Stir in cornbread mixture.
- Remove tops of tomatoes. Scoop out pulp and seeds. Invert to drain.
- Stuff mixture in tomatoes. Place in shallow pan.
- Bake uncovered about 20 minutes.
- Serve hot.

Serves 6

Zucchini and Tomatoes

2 pounds small zucchini	freshly ground white pepper to taste
6 tablespoons butter or margarine, divided	1 teaspoon finely chopped garlic
¼ cup finely chopped scallions	1 finely chopped green pepper
6 small ripe tomatoes, skinned, quartered and seeded	½ cup freshly grated Parmesan cheese
2 tablespoons olive oil salt to taste	2 tablespoons chopped, fresh parsley

- Wash the zucchini and cut them into horizontal slices about ½-inch thick. Put them in a boiler, cover with cold water and bring to a boil.
- Drain immediately and set them aside.
- Melt 2 tablespoons butter in a skillet.
- Add scallions and cook over low heat until they just turn brown.
- Spread the tomato sections on the onions and pour olive oil over them.
- Sprinkle with salt and pepper; add garlic and green pepper.
- Cover the skillet and cook the mixture over low heat for 10 minutes.
- Uncover the skillet and arrange the zucchini on the tomato mixture.
- Melt the remaining 4 tablespoons butter and sprinkle it over the zucchini.
- Cover the pan, and cook over low heat for 2-3 minutes.
- Turn the vegetables into a serving dish. Sprinkle with grated cheese and chopped parsley.

Serves 8

Chu-Chu's Vegetable Sauce

½ cup butter	2 cups sour cream
½ cup grated Parmesan cheese	¼ cup fresh, chopped chives
1 teaspoon salt	⅓ cup chopped cucumber

- Cream together butter, cheese and salt.
- Blend in sour cream, chives and cucumber.
- Spoon over hot green beans or serve with carrot sticks and cucumber slices.

Yields 3 cups

Simple Spicy Pasta

1 (8-ounce) package pasta
2 tablespoons olive oil
2 (16-ounce) cans Italian
   stewed tomatoes
1 teaspoon fresh basil
¼ teaspoon salt
¼ teaspoon pepper

1 clove grated garlic
1 tablespoon crushed chili
   pods
1 cup freshly grated
   mozzarella cheese
¾ cup freshly grated
   Parmesan cheese

- Stir raw pasta in olive oil in a large skillet until well coated and heated thoroughly.
- Add tomatoes, basil, salt, pepper, garlic and chili pods.
- Bring to a boil, then simmer until pasta is tender, stirring often.
- Sprinkle with mozzarella and Parmesan cheese.
- Serve immediately.

Serves 8

Fettucini Carbonara

4 beaten eggs
¼ cup butter
¼ cup whipping cream
8 ounces bacon, cut up
1 pound fettucini

1 cup fresh, grated Parmesan
   cheese
¼ cup fresh, chopped parsley
2 teaspoons ground
   peppercorns

- Let eggs, butter and cream stand at room temperature for 3 hours.
- Heat an ovenproof serving dish in a 250-degree oven.
- Cook bacon until brown. Drain.
- Beat together eggs and cream just until blended.
- Add pasta to boiling salted water. Cook 10-12 minutes. Drain.
- Turn hot pasta into heated dish. Toss pasta with butter.
- Pour cream mixture over pasta. Toss until pasta is well coated.
- Add bacon, cheese, parsley and peppercorns.
- Serve immediately.

Serves 6-8

Pasta with Broccoli and Pine Nuts

1	large bunch broccoli (2 pounds)		salt and pepper
2	tablespoons olive oil, divided	¾	pound whole-wheat spaghetti
2	minced cloves garlic	¼	cup freshly grated Parmesan cheese
¼	cup pine nuts	3	tablespoons fresh parsley

- Wash and break broccoli into florets.
- Steam until tender and still crisp.
- Refresh under cold water and set aside.
- Bring a large pot of water to a boil.
- Meanwhile heat 1 tablespoon of olive oil in a wide, heavy bottomed skillet over low heat and gently sauté the garlic and pine nuts until the garlic is golden.
- Add the broccoli and stir together over low heat until the broccoli is heated thoroughly.
- Set aside. Season to taste with salt and pepper.
- When the water comes to a boil, add 1 teaspoon salt, the remaining oil and the spaghetti.
- Cook the pasta and drain.
- Toss at once with the broccoli mixture.
- Add Parmesan cheese and parsley.
- Serve on warmed plates.

Serves 8

Mixed Fruit with Liqueurs

2	cups fresh strawberries	2	tablespoons orange-flavored liqueur
1	orange		
2	tablespoons orange juice	1	tablespoon cognac
3	tablespoons confectioners' sugar	1	tablespoon framboise (raspberry liqueur)

- Rinse and hull strawberries and place in mixing bowl.
- Peel orange and cut into sections, removing all seeds.
- Combine strawberries, oranges and orange juice and sprinkle with sugar.
- Refrigerate 1 hour or longer.
- When ready to serve, add liqueur, cognac and framboise. Toss well.

Serves 8

Chili and Corn Flan

½ cup canned, creamed corn
½ cup grated, sharp Cheddar
  cheese
½ cup cooked rice
¼ cup cornmeal
¼ cup milk
¼ cup sliced and pitted black
  olives

2 tablespoons chopped
  scallions
1 tablespoon seeded,
  deveined and chopped
  jalapeño chilies
1 tablespoon vegetable oil
1 beaten egg
½ teaspoon salt
⅛ teaspoon baking powder
1 drop hot pepper sauce

- Preheat oven to 350 degrees.
- Generously grease a 3-cup baking dish or ovenproof bowl.
- Mix corn, cheese, rice, cornmeal, milk, olives, scallions, jalapeño chilies, oil, egg, salt, baking powder and pepper sauce.
- Spoon into prepared dish.
- Bake until slightly puffed and lightly browned, about 30 minutes.
- Serve immediately.

Serves 2

Cranberry Apple Bake

3 cups apples
2 cups cranberries
½ cup sugar
⅓ cup brown sugar

¼ cup melted butter
1 cup oats
¼ cup brown sugar
½ cup chopped pecans

- Preheat oven to 350 degrees.
- Core, peel and chop apples.
- Pour apples, cranberries, sugar and ⅓ cup brown sugar into 9x13-inch dish.
- Mix together melted butter, oats, ¼ cup brown sugar and chopped pecans.
- Sprinkle on top of apple and cranberry mixture.
- Bake for 45 minutes.

Serves 6

El Paso Pilaf

½   cup chopped onion
2   teaspoons olive oil
1   (15-ounce) can dark red
    kidney beans
1¾ cups chicken broth
1   cup brown or white, long-
    grain rice
1   cup chunky salsa
¼   cup dry lentils, soaked,
    rinsed and drained

1   cup frozen yellow corn,
    thawed
¼   cup chopped red pepper
½   teaspoon chili powder
¼   teaspoon garlic powder
¼   cup chopped, fresh cilantro
    lemon pepper and garlic
    salt to taste
8   fresh, ripe tomato slices

- In a large saucepan sauté the onion in hot oil until tender, but not brown.
- Add beans, broth, rice, salsa, lentils, corn, red pepper, chili powder, garlic powder, cilantro, lemon pepper and garlic salt.
- Bring to a boil and reduce heat.
- Cover and simmer for 20 minutes or until lentils and rice are tender and most of the liquid is absorbed.
- Serve over fresh ripe tomatoes.
- Great with cornbread.

Serves 6

Orzo Salad

16 ounces orzo (1½ packages)
⅔   cup olive oil
⅓   cup lemon juice
½   teaspoon salt
¼   teaspoon pepper
¼   cup chopped scallions

2   tablespoons chopped, fresh
    parsley
6   ounces Feta cheese
4   tablespoons toasted pine
    nuts

- Cook orzo according to package directions.
- Rinse in cold water and cool. Set aside.
- Make dressing with olive oil, lemon juice, salt, pepper, scallions and parsley. Mix well.
- Crumble Feta cheese over the orzo. Add the pine nuts.
- Pour dressing over all and toss well.

Serves 4

Southwestern Rice

2 tablespoons butter	1 cup white, long-grain rice
1 finely chopped white onion, divided	2 cups chicken broth, divided
2 dry chili peppers, crushed	½ cup chopped, fresh cilantro

- Melt butter in large frying pan.
- Sauté ⅔ of the chopped onion.
- Stir in crushed peppers.
- When onion is clear and tender, stir in rice.
- Add 1 cup of chicken broth and simmer uncovered.
- As liquid is absorbed, add the second cup of broth, ½ cup at a time.
- Simmer about 20-25 minutes until rice is tender, but still a little chewy.
- During the last minute or so, stir in the remaining ⅓ of the onion and all the cilantro.
- Heat for 1 more minute.
- Serve hot.

Serves 6

Cinnamon Rice Mexican-Style

½ cup chopped onion	2¼ cups chicken broth
1 minced clove garlic	2 tablespoons ground cinnamon
2 tablespoons butter	¾ teaspoon minced, fresh cilantro
1 cup quick-cooking long-grain rice	
¼ cup raisins	

- In a saucepan over medium heat, cook the onion and garlic in butter until clear in color.
- Stir in rice, raisins, broth and cinnamon.
- Stir occasionally.
- Reduce heat and simmer for 5 minutes without stirring.
- Just before serving, fluff the rice, add cilantro and fluff again.
- Serve hot.

Serves 4

Nutty Citrus Rice

1	cup sliced scallions	¼	cup orange juice
½	cup chopped walnuts	1	teaspoon grated orange peel
½	cup golden raisins	½	teaspoon salt
1	tablespoon butter	½	teaspoon black pepper
3	cups cooked white, long-grain rice	1	can Mandarin orange segments, drained
1	cup cooked, wild rice		

- Sauté scallions, walnuts and raisins in butter over medium heat until scallions are tender.
- Add rice, wild rice, orange juice and orange peel.
- Add salt and pepper.
- Heat thoroughly.
- Gently stir in orange segments just before serving.

Serves 8

Company's Coming Rice

¼	cup cooking oil	1½	teaspoons salt
2	cups chopped, fresh parsley	3	beaten eggs
2	finely chopped bell peppers	2	cups milk
1	finely chopped clove garlic	2	cups freshly grated Cheddar cheese
3	finely chopped scallions	2	cups cooked white, long-grain rice

- Preheat oven to 325 degrees.
- Mix cooking oil, parsley, bell pepper, garlic, scallions, salt, eggs, milk and cheese.
- Blend mixture with rice.
- Pour into greased 9x13-inch pan.
- Bake for 45 minutes or until top is golden brown.

Serves 6

Heavenly Pasta and Rice Casserole

1   package angel hair pasta
½   cup butter
1   cup raw rice
1   cup chicken broth

1   (10½-ounce) can onion
     soup
2   tablespoons soy sauce
½   cup sliced and toasted
     almonds

- Preheat oven to 350 degrees.
- Brown raw pasta in butter until golden brown. Cook on very low heat. This tends to burn quickly.
- Add raw rice, chicken broth, onion soup and soy sauce.
- Cover and simmer until rice is done. This takes about 25 minutes.
- Turn into a 2-quart, buttered casserole.
- Sprinkle with almonds and bake uncovered for 30 minutes.

Serves 6

Egg-Bread Dressing

1   medium hen with giblets
1½   cups finely ground
       cornmeal
1   teaspoon baking soda
1   teaspoon salt
2   eggs
2   cups buttermilk

2   tablespoons corn oil
1   cup chopped onion
1   cup chopped celery
5-6 large eggs
4   slices white bread
     salt and pepper to taste

- Boil hen in large pan or Dutch oven.
- Reserve stock and giblets. Use hen for another purpose.
- Preheat oven to 450 degrees.
- Sift together cornmeal, baking soda and salt.
- In separate bowl, mix 2 eggs, buttermilk and oil. Add cornmeal mixture to this.
- Pour into greased shallow baking pan and bake for 20 minutes. Remove from oven and cool.
- Reduce heat to 350 degrees.
- In large bowl, mix egg-bread, stock from hen, giblets, onion, celery, eggs and bread. Use enough stock to form a very moist mixture.
- Pour into an 18x12x2½-inch baking pan and bake for 1 hour.
- Cool 15 minutes before serving.

Serves 12-15

Mushroom Rice

1 cup sliced onions	3 cups cooked, brown rice
½ pound sliced, fresh mushrooms	2½ cups beef broth (to cook rice)
3 tablespoons chopped, fresh parsley	¼ cup wheat germ
	¼ teaspoon fresh basil
3 tablespoons vegetable oil	½ teaspoon cumin seed

- Sauté onions, mushrooms and parsley in oil until tender.
- Cook rice in beef broth.
- Add cooked rice, wheat germ, fresh basil and cumin seed to onion mixture.
- Heat thoroughly, stirring constantly.
- Serve hot.

Serves 6

Mama's Cornbread Dressing

1 large chopped onion	6 hard-boiled eggs
2 stalks celery	2 teaspoons poultry seasoning
6 cups prepared cornbread (or 2 boxes commercial cornbread mix prepared)	3 chicken bouillon cubes
	3-4 cups hot water
6 slices stale or toasted, white bread	

- Preheat oven to 350 degrees.
- Boil onion and celery in small amount of water until tender.
- In large mixing bowl combine onions, celery, cornbread and white bread.
- Chop eggs and mix in bread mixture. Add poultry seasoning.
- Dissolve bouillon cubes in remaining water and add to bread mixture. The juicier this mixture is the better.
- Pour into a large baking pan (at least 12x9x2½-inch) and bake about 45 minutes. Top should be lightly browned.
- Serve with giblet gravy.

Serves 8-10

Giblet Gravy

giblets from 1 turkey
4-5 hard-boiled eggs
¼ cup bacon grease
2 tablespoons all-purpose
   flour

1 cup chicken or turkey
   broth
   salt and pepper

- In small heavy saucepan, boil giblets slowly for about 30 minutes.
- Drain, chop and reserve. Chop eggs and reserve.
- In same saucepan, heat grease over medium heat. Whisk in flour and stir until browned.
- Slowly add broth and, once incorporated smoothly, add giblets, eggs and salt and pepper to taste.
- Serve hot with cornbread dressing.

Yields 1 cup

Oyster Stuffing for 9- to 10-pound Turkey

1 cup butter, divided
½ cup chopped onion
3 cups chopped celery
½ cup chopped parsley
4 cups oysters
8 cups soft, white bread
   crumbs

4 cups soft, whole wheat
   bread crumbs
2 teaspoons salt
¼ teaspoon pepper
1 tablespoon poultry
   seasoning
¼ teaspoon mace
2 tablespoons lemon juice

- Put ½ cup butter in a large skillet. Sauté onion, celery and parsley for 5 minutes. Put in large bowl.
- Drain oysters well. Reserve liquid. Chop oysters coarsely.
- Sauté oysters in ½ cup butter for 3 minutes.
- Add to vegetable mixture oysters, bread, salt, pepper, poultry seasoning, mace, lemon juice and oyster juice to moisten. Toss lightly.
- Stuff into turkey and bake according to directions on turkey.

Yields 9 cups stuffing for 9- to 10-pound turkey

Buttercup

Breads

Buttercup
Gorham Corporation
Providence, Rhode Island

The fact that many early pieces of <u>Buttercup</u> are stamped with the date 1900 not withstanding, this pattern was actually introduced in 1899. The designer is unknown.

"An everlasting bouquet of delicate flowers intricately wrought in silver..." is the way <u>Buttercup</u> is described in an early Gorham catalog. The French-style handle is symmetrically decorated with masses and borders of buttercups in strong relief.

<u>Buttercup</u> is a perennially popular pattern.

For the history of Gorham, see the discussion under <u>Strasbourg</u>.

Pictured: English biscuit (cookie) box on stand, English butter spreader and <u>Buttercup</u> place setting

Applesauce Coffee Cake

2 cups self-rising flour
2 cups sugar
1 cup cooking oil
1 cup applesauce
1 teaspoon cinnamon

1 teaspoon cloves
3 eggs
1½ cups confectioners' sugar
   juice of 1 lemon

- Preheat oven to 350 degrees.
- Mix flour, sugar, oil, applesauce, cinnamon, cloves and eggs together.
- Pour in greased bundt pan.
- Bake for 1 hour.
- Mix confectioners' sugar and lemon juice together.
- Put on coffee cake while hot.
- Serve warm.

Serves 14-16

Banana Nut Bread

2¼ cups sifted all-purpose
    flour
1½ teaspoons baking powder
¾ teaspoon baking soda
1 teaspoon salt
1½ cups sugar
½ cup firmly packed brown
    sugar

¾ cup shortening
6 tablespoons buttermilk
1½ cups mashed, ripe bananas
    (about 3)
1½ teaspoons vanilla flavoring
3 eggs
¾ cup chopped nuts, dusted
    with 6 tablespoons flour

- Preheat oven to 350 degrees.
- Sift together flour, baking powder, soda, salt and sugar.
- Add brown sugar, shortening, buttermilk and bananas.
- Beat mixture for 2 minutes.
- Add vanilla and eggs and beat for 1 minute.
- Fold in nuts.
- Pour batter into a greased and floured bundt or tube pan.
- Bake for 1 hour.

Yields 14-16 servings

Blueberry Oat Muffins

2	cups blueberries	1	teaspoon salt
2	tablespoons all-purpose flour	½	cup cold butter
¾	cup old-fashioned oats (rolled oats)	1½	tablespoons grated lemon rind
1½	cups all-purpose flour	⅔	cup milk
1	cup sugar	1	egg
2	teaspoons double-acting baking powder	1½	tablespoons sugar
		2	teaspoons cinnamon

- Preheat oven to 400 degrees.
- Toss blueberries with 2 tablespoons flour.
- In blender or food processor, grind oats to a fine powder.
- Sift oat powder, 1½ cups flour, 1 cup sugar, baking powder and salt, and combine well.
- Cut butter into bits.
- Add butter and grated lemon rind to mixture.
- Blend mixture until it resembles meal.
- Add blueberries.
- In another bowl, lightly beat milk and egg.
- Add to flour mixture and stir until combined.
- In small bowl, mix 1½ tablespoons sugar and cinnamon.
- Grease muffin tins.
- Spoon batter into muffin tins until ⅔-full.
- Mix sugar and cinnamon together.
- Sprinkle sugar-cinnamon mixture on top of batter in muffin tins.
- Bake 20-25 minutes.

Yields 16 muffins

Cream Cheese Carrot Bread

1 (8-ounce) package softened
   cream cheese
1½ cups sugar
2 beaten eggs
2 tablespoons milk
1 teaspoon vanilla
2 cups all-purpose flour

1 teaspoon baking powder
1 teaspoon cinnamon
½ teaspoon baking soda
1½ cups shredded carrots
1 cup chopped pecans
¼ cup raisins

- Preheat oven to 350 degrees.
- Combine cream cheese and sugar, mixing until well blended.
- Blend in eggs, milk and vanilla.
- Combine flour, baking powder, cinnamon and baking soda and add to mixture, mixing until moistened.
- Stir in carrots, pecans and raisins.
- Pour into greased and floured 9x5-inch loaf pan.
- Bake for 1 hour or until done.
- Cool 10 minutes and remove from pan.

Yields 1 loaf

Chocolate Tea Bread

1¾ cups flour
1 teaspoon baking soda
½ teaspoon salt
½ cup butter
1 cup sugar
½ teaspoon vanilla

1 egg
1 teaspoon instant coffee
⅓ cup cocoa
1 cup buttermilk
1 cup halved, candied
   cherries
1½ cups chopped nuts

- Preheat oven to 350 degrees.
- Sift flour, baking soda and salt.
- Cream butter and add sugar and vanilla.
- Add egg, coffee and cocoa on low speed to creamed mixture.
- Slowly add buttermilk and dry ingredients.
- Stir in halved cherries and nuts.
- Bake in greased and floured loaf pan for 1 hour and 15 minutes.

Yields 1 loaf

Cranberry Banana Nut Bread

⅔ cup margarine
1½ cups sugar
3 eggs
2 cups mashed bananas
   (about 4)

3½ cups sifted self-rising flour
¼ teaspoon baking soda
1 cup chopped walnuts
1 (1-pound) can whole-berry
   cranberry sauce

- Preheat oven to 325 degrees.
- Cream margarine and sugar.
- Add eggs and beat.
- Stir in bananas, flour, baking soda and nuts.
- Fold in cranberry sauce.
- Pour into 3 greased and floured 9x5-inch loaf pans.
- Bake 45 minutes.
- This is excellent when served with Almond-Peach Butter.

Yields 3 loaves

Williamsburg Orange Muffins

2 cups all-purpose flour
1 teaspoon baking powder
½ cup margarine
2 cups sugar, divided
2 lightly beaten eggs

¾ cup buttermilk
1 cup golden raisins
1 cup chopped pecans
   juice and rind of 2 oranges
   and 1 lemon

- Preheat oven to 350 degrees.
- Sift flour and baking powder together.
- Cream margarine and 1 cup sugar.
- Add eggs to margarine and sugar.
- Add flour alternately with buttermilk to sugar mixture.
- Mix in raisins and pecans.
- Pour into greased or paper-lined mini muffin tins until ½-full.
- Bake for 15 minutes.
- Mix 1 cup sugar, juice of oranges and lemon and ¼ teaspoon orange and lemon rind.
- Pour sauce over muffins while still warm.

Yields 2 dozen

Sharon's Pumpkin Bread

3 cups sugar
1 cup salad oil
4 beaten eggs
1 (16-ounce) can pumpkin
3½ cups all-purpose flour
2 teaspoons baking soda
1 teaspoon salt
1 teaspoon baking powder

1 teaspoon nutmeg
1 teaspoon allspice
1 teaspoon cinnamon
½ teaspoon ground cloves
⅔ cup water
½ cup pecans (optional)
½ cup raisins (optional)

- Preheat oven to 350 degrees.
- Cream sugar and oil.
- Add eggs and pumpkin; mix well.
- Sift together flour, baking soda, salt, baking powder, nutmeg, allspice, cinnamon and cloves. Add sifted ingredients to batter alternately with water.
- Stir in pecans and/or raisins, if desired.
- Pour into well greased and floured loaf pan.
- Bake for 45 minutes.

Yields 2 large loaves or 4 small loaves

This recipe for pumpkin bread was given to me by Sharon DuBois of Birmingham, Alabama. Sharon was a wonderful cook and dear friend. She died of cancer several years ago, and each Fall I make this bread and remember all of the wonderful times we shared. So in her memory, I share it with you.
- Frances Sawyer

Almond-Peach Butter

½ cup softened butter or margarine
⅓ cup peach preserves

½ teaspoon almond extract
1 tablespoon confectioners' sugar

- Whip butter with electric mixer until smooth and fluffy.
- Add preserves, extract and confectioners' sugar.
- Store in refrigerator.

Yields ½ pint

Pecan Bread

1¼ cups self-rising flour	4 eggs
2 cups sugar	2 teaspoons vanilla
½ cup melted butter	2 cups chopped pecans

- Preheat oven to 350 degrees.
- Mix flour, sugar, butter, eggs, vanilla and pecans together well.
- Pour into 2 well greased cake or pie pans.
- Bake for 20-30 minutes.
- After bread has cooled, stack together and serve.

Serves 12

This Pecan Bread became a favorite of our cookbook committee. We enjoyed many different versions of the recipe during our lengthy, but fun, committee meetings. Chunky apricot preserves created a wonderful filling when spread between the two layers. A dusting of confectioners' sugar made our time together complete.

Strawberry Bread

3 cups all-purpose flour	1¼ cups chopped pecans
1 teaspoon salt	2 (10-ounce) packages frozen
2 cups sugar	strawberries, thawed
1 teaspoon baking soda	1¼ cups cooking oil
3 teaspoons cinnamon	3 beaten eggs

- Preheat oven to 350 degrees.
- Sift flour, salt, sugar, baking soda and cinnamon in a large mixing bowl.
- Make a well in center of dry ingredients.
- Mix pecans, strawberries, cooking oil and eggs and pour into well.
- Stir enough to dampen all ingredients.
- Pour into 2 large, greased loaf pans.
- Bake for 1 hour.

Yields 2 loaves

Zucchini Nut Bread

3   eggs
1   cup oil
2½ cups sugar
2   cups peeled and grated
    zucchini
3   teaspoons vanilla

3   cups all-purpose flour
1   teaspoon salt
1   teaspoon baking soda
1   teaspoon baking powder
3   teaspoons cinnamon
½   cup chopped nuts

- Preheat oven to 325 degrees.
- Beat eggs.
- Add oil, sugar, zucchini and vanilla. Mix lightly, but well.
- Add flour, salt, baking soda, baking powder, cinnamon and nuts, and beat well.
- Pour into 2 greased loaf pans.
- Bake for 1 hour.

Yields 2 loaves

Jalapeño Cornbread

1½ cups yellow cornmeal
3   teaspoons baking powder
½   teaspoon salt
1   cup grated Longhorn
    Cheddar cheese
1   cup grated onion

5   large jalapeño peppers,
    seeded and finely
    chopped
3   lightly beaten eggs
½   cup oil
1   cup sour cream
1   (8½-ounce) can cream-style
    corn

- Preheat oven to 400 degrees.
- Mix cornmeal, baking powder and salt.
- Add cheese, onion and peppers.
- Add eggs, oil, sour cream and corn and stir well.
- Grease a large cast iron skillet and heat in oven until hot or use muffin tins.
- Pour batter in pan or tins.
- Bake 20-30 minutes.

Serves 12

Best Cornbread

½ cup vegetable oil
1 (8-ounce) carton sour
    cream
2 eggs

1 cup self-rising, yellow
    cornmeal
1 teaspoon salt
1 (8-ounce) can cream-style
    corn

- Preheat oven to 400 degrees.
- Cream oil and sour cream.
- Add eggs, cornmeal, salt and corn and mix.
- Pour into hot, greased muffin pan or corn stick pan.
- Bake 25-30 minutes.

Yields 12 muffins or corn sticks

Onion Cornbread

2 cups finely chopped onion
¼ cup melted butter or
    margarine
1½ cups self-rising cornmeal
2 tablespoons sugar
¼ teaspoon dill weed
1 cup shredded Cheddar
    cheese, divided

2 well beaten eggs
¼ cup milk
¼ cup vegetable oil
1 (8-ounce) carton sour
    cream
1 (8¾-ounce) can cream-style
    corn
   dash hot pepper sauce
   (optional)

- Preheat oven to 400 degrees.
- Sauté onion in butter.
- Combine cornmeal, sugar and dill weed.
- Add onion, ½ cup cheese, eggs, milk, vegetable oil, sour cream and corn. Add hot pepper sauce, if desired.
- Stir well until moist.
- Spoon into 10-inch iron skillet.
- Bake for 20 minutes.
- Sprinkle with remaining ½ cup cheese.
- Bake until cheese is lightly browned.

Serves 12

Greek Cinnamon Logs

2 cups sugar, divided	2 egg yolks
1 tablespoon cinnamon	2 giant loaves sliced, white
2 (8-ounce) packages	bread
softened cream cheese	1 cup melted butter

- Mix 1 cup sugar and cinnamon; set aside.
- Blend cream cheese, egg yolks and 1 cup sugar until smooth.
- Trim crust off bread and roll flat.
- Spread cheese filling on bread.
- Roll bread up, dip in butter and roll in cinnamon/sugar mixture.
- Wrap in foil and freeze for 24 hours.
- Preheat oven to 350 degrees.
- Before cooking, take out of foil and cut in thirds.
- Bake on greased or non-stick cookie sheets for 15 minutes.

Yields 14 dozen

English Muffin Loaf

6 cups all-purpose flour, divided	¼ teaspoon baking soda
2 packages active, dry yeast	2 cups milk
1 tablespoon sugar	½ cup water
2 teaspoons salt	cornmeal

- Heat milk and water to 120 degrees.
- Combine 3 cups flour, yeast, sugar, salt and baking soda.
- Stir liquids into dry ingredients. Stir in enough of the remaining flour to make a stiff batter.
- Grease 2 loaf pans and sprinkle with cornmeal.
- Divide batter into pans. Sprinkle with cornmeal. Cover and let rise 45 minutes.
- Preheat oven to 400 degrees.
- Bake uncovered for 25 minutes.
- Remove from pans immediately.
- Store in refrigerator.

Yields 2 loaves

Herb Bread

½ cup milk	2¼ cups white or whole wheat
1½ tablespoons sugar	flour
1 teaspoon salt	½ small, minced onion
1 tablespoon butter	½ teaspoon dried dill weed
1 package active, dry yeast	1 teaspoon crushed, dried
½ cup warm water	rosemary

- Scald milk and dissolve sugar, salt and butter into milk. Cool to lukewarm.
- Dissolve yeast in warm water and add to cool milk with flour, onion, dill weed and rosemary.
- Stir well with a wooden spoon. When batter is smooth, cover with a towel and let rise in warm spot until triple in bulk (45-60 minutes).
- Preheat oven to 350 degrees.
- Stir down and beat a few minutes, then turn into greased bread pan. Let stand in warm spot 10 minutes.
- Bake for 50 minutes.

Yields 1 loaf

Break Away Bread

2 packages active, dry yeast	¾ cup sugar
1 cup warm water	1½ teaspoons salt
1 cup boiling water	2 eggs, beaten
1 cup margarine	7 cups bread flour

- Mix yeast and warm water; set aside.
- In large bowl, pour boiling water over margarine. Stir until dissolved.
- Add sugar, salt and eggs to yeast mixture. Stir in flour.
- Place lid on bowl and store in refrigerator overnight.
- Divide dough in half and roll out to ¼-inch thickness and cut with biscuit cutter.
- Dip each biscuit in melted butter and stack in greased bundt pan.
- Let rise 2 hours or until doubled in size.
- Preheat and bake in oven at 350 degrees for 20 minutes.
- Dough will last in refrigerator for up to 3 days.

Serves 16-20

Pesto Bread

2	packages active, dry yeast	5-5½	cups flour, divided
1	cup warm water	2	cups fresh basil leaves, washed and dried
1	tablespoon sugar		
4	eggs	4	garlic cloves
½	cup oil	1	cup walnuts or pecans
¼	cup sugar	1	cup olive oil
¼	cup butter, room temperature	1¼	cups Parmesan cheese salt and pepper to taste
2	teaspoons salt	1	lightly beaten egg white

- Dissolve yeast in warm water with 1 tablespoon of sugar added.
- Mix eggs, oil, ¼ cup sugar, butter and salt.
- Add 2¼ cups flour and mix well. Add yeast and enough flour to make a soft dough.
- Turn onto floured surface and knead until smooth and elastic (8-10 minutes).
- Place dough into greased bowl, turning to coat entire surface. Cover with cloth and let rise until double, about 1½ hours.
- Punch down in bowl and divide into 2 parts. Roll dough into rectangle.
- To make pesto sauce, combine basil, garlic and nuts in food processor. Leave motor running and slowly add oil.
- Turn off motor and add cheese, salt and pepper.
- Spread ¼ cup pesto sauce onto dough. Roll dough up like a jelly roll and coil into a circle. Brush surface with egg white.
- Repeat with remaining dough.
- Place on baking pan and cover and let rise until double, about 45 minutes.
- Bake 350 degrees for 30 minutes until dough sounds hollow when tapped.
- Cool on racks.

Yields 2 loaves

Use bottled or distilled water in yeast recipes. The chemicals in your tap water could destroy the yeast.

Bubble Wreath Coffee Cake

¼ cup water
1 package active, dry yeast
¼ cup + 1 tablespoon sugar, divided
1 cup milk
¼ cup shortening
3½ cups flour, divided (may need ¼ cup more)
1 egg

2 tablespoons butter
2 tablespoons corn syrup
½ cup brown sugar
16 cherry halves or ½ cup raisins
¼ cup pecan pieces
½ cup melted butter
1 teaspoon cinnamon
1 cup sugar

- In small bowl, combine warm water, yeast and 1 tablespoon sugar. Let sit 5 minutes. This mixture should bubble. If not, start over with new yeast.
- Scald milk. Cool to warm. Add ¼ cup sugar and shortening.
- Add 2 cups of flour to milk. Mix well.
- Mix yeast mixture and egg into flour mixture. Beat 2-3 minutes until well mixed.
- Stir in (by hand) enough of remaining flour to make stiff dough.
- Turn out on a lightly floured surface and knead dough for 5 minutes until smooth and elastic.
- Place dough in a greased bowl, turning once to grease the dough. Cover and let rise until it doubles, about 2 hours.
- Grease 10-inch tube pan. Mix 2 tablespoons butter, corn syrup and brown sugar. Spread in bottom of pan.
- Place cherry halves and pecans on top of sugar mixture.
- Make 48 balls out of dough. Roll balls in melted butter.
- Mix cinnamon and sugar and roll balls in mixture. Place in layers in pan.
- Let rise 45 minutes.
- Preheat oven to 400 degrees and bake for 35 minutes. Loosen coffee cake from pan and turn out quickly. (Do not let cake cool in pan.)

Serves 16

Herb-Onion Rolls

2 packages active, dry yeast	1 teaspoon fresh oregano, crushed
1/3 cup nonfat, dry milk powder	1/2 teaspoon fresh tarragon, crumbled
2 tablespoons honey	1/4 cup vegetable oil
1 tablespoon salt	1 cup warm milk
1 small, minced onion	1 cup very warm water
1 teaspoon fresh basil, crumbled	2 cups whole wheat flour
	1½ cups all-purpose flour

- Combine yeast, dry milk, honey, salt and onion.
- Grind basil, oregano and tarragon in coffee grinder.
- Add to yeast mixture. Add oil. Stir in warm milk and water. Beat until well blended.
- Blend flours.
- Stir 2 cups flour mixture into yeast mixture. Beat with electric mixer at medium speed for 2 minutes.
- Stir in another cup of flour mixture and beat 1 minute.
- Beat in remaining flour mixture by hand until heavy, sticky dough forms.
- Fill 18 well greased muffin pan cups.
- Push dough down, smoothing tops slightly.
- Cover with cloth and let rise 20 minutes.
- Bake in preheated oven at 375 degrees for 20 minutes or until rolls sound hollow when tapped.
- Remove from pan and cool on wire racks.

Yields 18 rolls

English Tea Spoon with Ivory Handle

Grandmother's Cinnamon Rolls

1 package active, dry yeast	⅓ cup warm milk
½ cup warm water	2½ cups all-purpose flour
3 tablespoons sugar	4 tablespoons melted butter, divided
4 tablespoons vegetable shortening	⅓ cup brown sugar
1 teaspoon salt	2 tablespoons cinnamon

- Dissolve yeast in large bowl with water and a sprinkle of sugar.
- Add sugar, shortening, salt and milk. Mix well. Add flour to make a soft dough.
- Put in a bowl sprayed with no-stick spray. Cover and let rise 1½ hours or until double in bulk.
- Roll dough on floured surface.
- Dot with 1 tablespoon butter; sprinkle generously with sugar and cinnamon.
- Roll up jelly-roll-style. Cut into 1-inch rounds.
- Combine remaining melted butter and brown sugar and pour into baking dish.
- Place rolls on top. Cover and let rise 1 hour.
- Preheat oven and bake at 400 degrees for 20 minutes or until golden brown.
- When done, turn upside down so that butter and sugar run down buns.
- For freezing, remove rolls from oven before browning.

Yields 1½ dozen

French Toast

1 cup all-purpose flour	1 cup milk
2 teaspoons sugar	1 egg
1½ teaspoons baking powder	8 slices stale bread
½ teaspoon salt	cooking oil
¼ teaspoon cinnamon	

- Blend flour, sugar, baking powder, salt and cinnamon.
- Mix milk and eggs together and add to dry ingredients.
- Dip bread in batter and fry in 1-2 inches of hot cooking oil until brown.
- Drain on paper towels.

Yields 8 slices

Monterey French Bread

8 ounces grated Monterey Jack cheese with jalapeño peppers	½ cup mayonnaise dash of garlic salt
½ cup butter	1 loaf French bread, sliced or 6 mini-loaves

- Preheat oven to 350 degrees.
- Cream cheese, butter, mayonnaise and garlic salt. Spread over sliced French bread (on both sides and on crust).
- Cover with foil.
- Bake for 30 minutes.

Serves 12

Orange Rolls

1 package active, dry yeast	¼ cup shortening
¼ cup warm water	2½ cups flour
¼ cup lukewarm milk, scalded, then cooled	3 tablespoons butter
¼ cup sugar	1 tablespoon grated orange peel
½ teaspoon salt	2 tablespoons orange juice
1 egg	1½ cups confectioners' sugar

- Dissolve yeast in warm water.
- Stir in milk, sugar, salt, egg, shortening and ½ of the flour. Beat until smooth. Mix in remaining flour.
- Knead dough 5 minutes.
- Place in greased bowl and cover, let rise until doubled, about 1½ hours. Punch down dough.
- Roll into 12x7-inch rectangle pan.
- Combine butter, orange peel, orange juice and confectioners' sugar.
- Spread dough with ½ of orange filling.
- Roll up beginning with wide side. Pinch to seal.
- Cut into 12 slices.
- Place in a greased, round 9-inch cake pan. Let rise until double.
- Preheat oven to 400 degrees and bake 12-18 minutes.
- While warm, frost with remaining filling.

Yields 12 rolls

Yeast Rolls

1 cup sugar
1 cup vegetable oil
4 cups milk
2 packages active, dry yeast
¼ cup warm water

8 cups flour, divided
1 teaspoon baking powder
1 teaspoon baking soda
1 heaping tablespoon salt
vegetable oil to brush on rolls

- Scald sugar, oil and milk. Cool to lukewarm.
- Add yeast to warm water.
- Add yeast mixture to cooled sugar mixture.
- Add 3 cups flour until dough is spongy. Dough will be very liquid. Let rise for 2 hours.
- Mix baking powder and soda, salt and 1 cup flour together, then add to dough mixture.
- Work in 3-4 cups of remaining flour until dough is firm, but still sticky.
- Roll out dough with rolling pin and cut with 2-inch cutter.
- Oil each roll and fold in half.
- Place on greased pan. Allow to rise for 1 hour.
- Preheat oven to 400 degrees and bake for 12-15 minutes until lightly browned.

Yields 5-6 dozen

Homemade Tortillas

3 cups flour
1 teaspoon baking powder
6 tablespoons shortening

¾ cup water (may need a little more)

- Put flour and baking powder in a bowl.
- Add shortening and mix well.
- Add water and mix completely.
- Knead until smooth.
- Pick small amount out and roll into a ball. (It should be the size of a small meatball.)
- Roll out as thin as possible in a circular form.
- Cook in a very hot black iron skillet.

Yields 6 tortillas

Grand Baroque

Desserts

Grand Baroque
Wallace International Silversmiths
Wallingford, Connecticut

Introduced in 1941, Grand Baroque was designed by William S. Warren. Warren's trademark was flatware with a three-dimensional design. Grand Baroque has a terminal featuring leaves, flowers and scrolls in high relief, the scroll work being accentuated by piercing. This ornate terminal contrasts sharply with the simple rounded stem. The design has a highly delineated three-dimensionality which can be appreciated from any side or view. It has been a best-seller since its introduction.

Wallace Silversmiths' origins go back to Robert Wallace, a spoonmaker who in 1834 acquired the formula for German nickel silver, an alloy not containing silver at all but much superior to the pewter commonly used for making every day spoons at that time. This company produced nickel silver spoons for various other companies for many years and eventually broadened out to produce silverplated and sterling flatware as well. In the 1950's, Wallace bought the Watson Company and the Tuttle Silver Company. Since 1959, Wallace itself has been bought out several times. The company is now a part of the International silverware conglomerate.

Pictured: Dutch pastry server, Lily American cake breaker by Whiting, Grand Baroque place setting and American pastry server

Almond-Stuffed Apples

½   cup blanched almonds
2   tablespoons water
1¼ cups sugar, divided
¼   teaspoon almond extract
8   medium, baking apples
½   cup melted butter

2   cups sifted, fine bread
    crumbs
½   pint whipping cream
⅓   cup confectioners' sugar
1   teaspoon vanilla

- Preheat oven to 425 degrees.
- Blend nuts in electric blender until finely ground.
- Add water, ¼ cup sugar and almond extract; blend until smooth.
- Peel and core apples; fill with almond paste.
- Roll apples in butter, bread crumbs and remaining sugar.
- Arrange apples in buttered baking dish.
- Bake for 25 minutes or until tender.
- Beat whipping cream, confectioners' sugar and vanilla until fluffy.
- Top baked apples with whipped cream and serve from baking dish.

Serves 8

Ruby Strawberries

1   (10-ounce) package frozen
    raspberries, thawed
½   cup sugar, divided
1   tablespoon lemon juice
1   teaspoon grated orange
    zest

1   tablespoon orange-flavored
    liqueur
1   quart strawberries
⅓   cup toasted, slivered
    almonds

- Press raspberries through a food mill or strainer to extract seeds.
- Mix raspberry liquid, ¼ cup sugar, lemon juice, grated orange zest and orange liqueur and stir.
- Combine strawberries and ¼ cup sugar.
- Pour raspberry sauce over strawberries and chill 4 hours.
- Top each serving with slivered almonds.

Serves 6-8

Frozen Peach Dessert

1 (8-ounce) carton sour cream
½ cup sugar
1 cup fresh, puréed peaches (about 4)

¾ cup + 2 tablespoons vanilla wafer crumbs
½ cup softened butter
2 cups sifted confectioners' sugar
2 large eggs

- Beat sour cream about 5 minutes, until fluffy.
- Continue beating while adding ½ cup sugar.
- Fold peaches into sour cream mixture.
- Spread ¾ cup vanilla wafer crumbs over bottom of 8-inch square pan.
- Cover with peach mixture and freeze until firm.
- Cream butter and gradually add confectioners' sugar. Beat until light.
- Add eggs, 1 at a time, beating well after each egg.
- Spread over peach layer.
- Sprinkle with 2 tablespoons vanilla wafer crumbs.
- Cover and freeze.

Serves 8

Apple Dumplings

1 cup sugar
1 cup orange juice
½ cup margarine

2 Granny Smith apples
1 can crescent rolls (8)

- Preheat oven to 350 degrees.
- Combine sugar, orange juice and margarine in a saucepan. Stir slowly and boil until sugar dissolves.
- Peel, core and quarter apples.
- Separate rolls.
- Wrap up ¼ apple in each roll and place in baking dish.
- Pour orange juice mixture evenly over apples.
- Cover with aluminum foil.
- Bake for 20 minutes.
- Remove foil and bake 15 more minutes.
- Serve warm if possible

Serves 8

White Chocolate Mousse

¾ cup sugar
⅜ cup water
    pinch cream of tartar
4   egg whites

½   pound finely-chopped
     white chocolate (not
     almond bark)
1   pint whipping cream
2½ ounces orange-flavored
     liqueur

- Combine sugar, water and cream of tartar in a small saucepan and cook to 230 degrees. This takes about 18 minutes.
- Just before temperature reaches 230 degrees, beat egg whites into stiff peaks.
- Slowly drizzle sugar mixture into egg whites while beating them.
- By hand, fold white chocolate into egg and sugar mixture.
- Place mixture in freezer.
- Whip cream and add orange-flavored liqueur. Then fold into chocolate mixture by hand.
- Put into individual parfait glasses.
- Freeze at least 1 hour before serving.
- Serve with raspberry sauce.

Raspberry Sauce

12 ounces raspberries, fresh
     or frozen

⅛   cup cornstarch, mixed with
     a little warm water to
     dissolve

- In a small saucepan, bring berries to a boil.
- Remove from heat and strain through a fine mesh strainer.
- Bring to a boil once more.
- Add cornstarch mixture.
- Remove from heat and cool.
- Serve sauce over each mousse.

Yields 12 (½-cup) servings

Amaretto Bread Pudding

1	quart half-and-half	10	tablespoons butter, divided
3	eggs	1	cup confectioners' sugar
1½	cups sugar	1	beaten egg
2	tablespoons almond extract	4	tablespoons almond-
1	loaf French bread		flavored liqueur

- In a large bowl, mix half-and-half, 3 eggs, sugar and extract.
- Tear bread into small pieces and add to mixture.
- Let stand for 1 hour.
- Preheat oven to 325 degrees.
- Grease 9x13x2-inch pan with 2 tablespoons melted butter.
- Pour bread mixture into pan and bake for 50 minutes.
- In top of a double boiler, cook remaining butter, sugar and 1 beaten egg over simmering water until very hot.
- Remove from heat and whisk mixture until it comes to room temperature.
- Whisk in almond-flavored liqueur.
- To serve, cut bread pudding into squares and spoon sauce over top.
- Run under broiler until sauce bubbles.

Serves 12

Bourbon Ice Cream Parfait

1	(8-ounce) bottle maraschino cherries bourbon	20	crisp macaroons or coconut cookies
		½	gallon vanilla ice cream
		1	cup chopped pecans

- Drain cherries, cut in halves and place in a glass measuring cup.
- Add bourbon to cherries to 8-ounce level and marinate overnight.
- Crumble cookies.
- Soften ice cream just enough to mix with cherries, bourbon, cookies and pecans.
- Spoon into 9 parfait glasses and place in freezer.

Serves 9

Bread and Butter Custard

2 cups heavy cream	¼ cup orange-flavored
2 cups milk	liqueur
3 strips orange peel	4 (½-inch thick) slices
6 egg yolks	French bread
3 whole eggs	confectioners' sugar
½ cup sugar	nutmeg

- Preheat oven to 325 degrees.
- Place heavy cream, milk and orange peel in a saucepan and bring to a boil.
- Let cook for 5 minutes.
- Place egg yolks and eggs in a large bowl.
- Add sugar and beat to a light cream color.
- Add orange-flavored liqueur and stir in cream mixture, discarding orange peel.
- Pour into a lightly greased 2-quart baking dish.
- Trim and butter French bread so that pieces float butter side up without overlapping.
- Place dish in a larger baking pan and pour boiling water to reach halfway up the sides.
- Bake 40-45 minutes until knife inserted comes out clean.
- Let cool and dust with confectioners' sugar and nutmeg.
- Best if served slightly warm.

Serves 6

Peachy Raspberry Sherbet

2 cups fresh or frozen peach slices	1 cup milk
¾ cup fresh or frozen raspberries	2 tablespoons honey
	½ teaspoon vanilla
	mint

- Reserve a few peach slices and raspberries for garnishing.
- In a food processor, blend milk, honey, vanilla and remaining peaches and raspberries until smooth.
- Spoon into 4 dessert dishes and freeze until firm.
- Garnish with fresh mint and reserved fruit.

Serves 4

Frozen Soufflé with Hot Strawberry Sauce

½ gallon vanilla ice cream
12 crumbled macaroons
10 tablespoons orange-
   flavored liqueur, divided
2 cups heavy cream
½ cup chopped, toasted
   almonds

confectioners' sugar
1 quart fresh strawberries or
   3 (10-ounce) packages
   frozen, sliced
   strawberries, thawed
½ cup sugar

- Soften ice cream slightly.
- Stir in crumbled macaroons and 5 tablespoons orange-flavored liqueur.
- Whip heavy cream until thick and shiny.
- Fold into ice cream mixture.
- Spoon into an angel food cake pan.
- Sprinkle surface lightly with almonds and confectioners' sugar and cover with plastic wrap.
- Freeze until firm.
- Wash, hull and halve fresh strawberries
- Put berries in saucepan and add sugar.
- Simmer until soft but not mushy.
- Remove from heat and stir in remaining orange-flavored liqueur.
- Unmold soufflé onto a cold platter.
- Serve soufflé topped with hot strawberry sauce.

Serves 10

18th Century, English Spoon by Anne and Peter Bateman

Chocolate Soufflé

3	tablespoons butter	½	cup sugar
2	tablespoons all-purpose flour	1	vanilla bean
1	cup milk	5	medium eggs, separated
2	squares baking chocolate		whipped cream
½	teaspoon salt		cognac

- Preheat oven to 400 degrees.
- Melt butter in a saucepan and blend thoroughly with the flour.
- Slowly add 1 cup milk, stirring constantly.
- Add chocolate, stirring until it is melted and sauce is thoroughly blended.
- Stir in the salt, sugar and vanilla bean.
- When sauce is smooth and thick, remove from heat and set aside.
- Remove vanilla bean.
- When cool, add lightly beaten egg yolks and beat thoroughly.
- Fold in 5 stiffly beaten egg whites.
- Butter a soufflé dish and sprinkle with a heavy coating of granulated sugar.
- Carefully spoon soufflé into dish and place in a large baking pan with 2 inches of hot water in the pan.
- Bake for 15 minutes.
- Reduce oven to 375 degrees and bake for 20-25 minutes longer.
- Serve with whipped cream.
- Drizzle a couple of drops of cognac over the whipped cream, if desired.

Serves 8

Pralines and Cream

½ cup oatmeal
½ cup light brown sugar
1 cup margarine
1 cup chopped nuts
2 cups all-purpose flour

2 (12-ounce) jars caramel topping
½ gallon softened, vanilla ice cream

- Preheat oven to 350 degrees.
- Combine oatmeal, sugar, margarine, nuts and flour.
- Bake for 20 minutes, stirring every 5 minutes.
- Cool this crunch mixture.
- Pack ½ of this mixture into a 9x15-inch pan.
- Pour 1 jar of caramel topping over crunch mixture.
- Spread softened ice cream on top of caramel layer.
- Pour second jar of caramel topping over ice cream.
- Top with remaining crunch mixture.
- Freeze until firm.
- Cut in squares to serve.

Serves 20

Buttermilk Custard Pie

½ cup softened butter
1½ cups sugar
3 tablespoons all-purpose flour
3 eggs

1 cup buttermilk
1 teaspoon lemon flavoring
pinch salt
1 (9-inch) baked pie shell

- Preheat oven to 450 degrees.
- Cream butter, gradually add sugar and beat well.
- Add flour and beat until smooth.
- Add eggs, and beat until mixed.
- Stir in buttermilk, lemon flavoring and salt and beat well.
- Pour mixture into baked pie shell.
- Bake for 15 minutes.
- Reduce oven temperature to 350 degrees and bake an additional 45 minutes or until set.

Serves 6-8

Foolproof Flan

1 cup sugar	1 can sweetened, condensed milk
1 (8-ounce) package softened cream cheese	1 can evaporated milk
	6 beaten eggs

- Preheat oven to 350 degrees.
- In a small iron skillet, brown sugar slowly on low heat until it is the consistency of syrup and a clear, light brown color. Make sure all sugar is dissolved.
- In a blender or mixer, beat softened cream cheese gently adding condensed milk, evaporated milk and eggs until well blended.
- Pour syrup mixture in the bottom of a flan or pie pan. Spread this evenly over the bottom of the pan.
- Gently pour flan mixture over this.
- Place flan pan into a larger pan filled with at least 1 inch of water for baking.
- Bake for 35 minutes.
- Cool overnight in refrigerator.
- Loosen sides with knife and invert onto a serving platter.
- Cut in wedges.
- This is really pretty on a crystal cake stand garnished with fresh pansies.

Serves 8

Depression Cracker Pie

3   egg whites
½   teaspoon cream of tartar
1   cup sugar
1   teaspoon vanilla extract
18 crumbled saltine crackers

1   cup chopped pecans
1   (9-ounce) carton whipped
    topping
1   cup frozen, sweetened
    strawberries, drained

• Preheat oven to 325 degrees.
• Beat eggs until fluffy.
• Add cream of tartar and beat until stiff.
• Add sugar and vanilla and beat until well blended.
• Fold in cracker crumbs and nuts.
• Spread in buttered 9-inch pie plate.
• Bake for 30 minutes. Cool.
• Mix whipped topping and strawberries.
• Spread over pie.
• Chill.

Serves 6

Strawberry Cream Pie

2   cups milk, divided
¼   cup all-purpose flour
½   cup sugar
⅛   teaspoon salt
2   tablespoons cornstarch

2   beaten egg yolks
1   (9-inch) baked pie shell
1   quart fresh strawberries
1   cup heavy, whipped cream

• Scald 1½ cups milk; remove from heat.
• Combine flour, sugar, salt and cornstarch.
• Blend with ½ cup cold milk.
• Blend scalded milk with flour mixture.
• Cook in top of double boiler, stirring constantly, until thick, about
  15 minutes.
• Whisk egg yolks into this mixture and cook about 2 minutes.
• Pour into baked shell and allow filling to set.
• Just before serving, wash, hull and slice strawberries.
• Cover pie with strawberries and top with sweetened whipped cream.
• Garnish with whole strawberries.

Serves 6-8

Christmas Chocolate-Pecan Fudge Pie

1¼ cups chocolate wafer
 crumbs
⅓ cup melted butter
½ cup softened butter or
 margarine
¾ cup firmly packed brown
 sugar
3 eggs
1 (12-ounce) package melted
 semi-sweet chocolate
 morsels

2 teaspoons instant coffee
 granules
1 teaspoon vanilla extract
½ cup all-purpose flour
1 cup coarsely chopped
 pecans
Garnishes: sweetened
 whipped cream,
 chocolate syrup,
 maraschino cherries with
 stems and mint sprigs

- Preheat oven to 350 degrees.
- Combine chocolate crumbs and ⅓ cup melted butter.
- Press firmly in 9-inch pie pan.
- Bake for 6-8 minutes.
- Increase oven to 375 degrees.
- Cream ½ cup butter with electric mixer at medium speed; gradually
  add brown sugar.
- Add eggs, one a time, beating well after each egg.
- Stir in melted chocolate, coffee granules, vanilla, flour and pecans.
- Pour mixture in crust.
- Bake for 25 minutes.
- Cool on rack.
- Garnish with whipped cream, chocolate syrup, cherries and mint.

Serves 6-8

Miniature Tarts

1 cup unsalted butter	1 teaspoon vanilla
1 teaspoon salt	1 egg
⅓ cup sugar	2½ cups all-purpose flour

- Process butter, salt and sugar in food processor.
- Add vanilla, egg and flour. Process until ball forms.
- Refrigerate dough 4 hours.
- Press 1 teaspoon dough into mini tart pans.
- Bake at 375 degrees for 10-12 minutes.
- Cool and fill with lemon curd or fudge filling.

Lemon Curd

10 egg yolks	¾ cup lemon juice
½ cup sugar	½ cup unsalted butter

- Combine egg yolks, sugar and lemon juice in heavy saucepan, over medium heat.
- Whisk slowly until almost boiling and remove from heat.
- Cut butter into pieces and add to saucepan. Stir until melted.
- Chill.
- Spoon into cooled tart shells prior to serving.

Fudge Filling

1 can sweetened, condensed milk	2 tablespoons butter
1 can chocolate syrup	1 teaspoon vanilla

- Combine sweetened, condensed milk, chocolate syrup and butter in top of double boiler.
- Heat, stirring often until mixture thickens.
- Add vanilla.
- Chill.
- Spoon into tart shells prior to serving.

Yields 7 dozen tart shells and filling for 10 dozen shells

Peaches and Cream Pie

3   cups fresh, sliced peaches
1   (9-inch) unbaked, deep
      dish pie shell
1½ cups sugar, divided
⅓ cup + ½ cup all-purpose
      flour, divided

⅛ teaspoon salt
1   beaten egg
½ cup sour cream
¼ cup butter or margarine

- Preheat oven to 350 degrees.
- Place peaches in bottom of pie shell.
- Combine 1 cup sugar, ⅓ cup flour and salt.
- Add egg and sour cream and blend well.
- Spoon over peaches.
- Combine remaining ½ cup sugar and ½ cup flour.
- Cut in butter until mixture resembles coarse meal and sprinkle evenly over pie.
- Bake for 55 minutes or until golden brown.
- Garnish with sliced fresh peaches.

Serves 8

Frozen Pumpkin Pie

1½ cups graham cracker
      crumbs
2¾ tablespoons sugar
⅓ cup melted margarine
1   quart softened vanilla ice
      cream
1   cup pumpkin
1⅛ cups sugar

1½ teaspoons cinnamon
½ teaspoon ginger
¼ teaspoon salt
½ teaspoon nutmeg
⅛ teaspoon ground cloves
1   cup whipping cream,
      whipped

- Preheat oven to 350 degrees.
- Mix graham cracker crumbs, sugar and margarine.
- Press into 9-inch pie pan.
- Bake for 8 minutes. Cool.
- Spoon ice cream into baked pie shell and freeze until firm.
- Blend pumpkin with sugar, cinnamon, ginger, salt, nutmeg and cloves.
- Fold in whipped cream.
- Spread over ice cream.
- Freeze until ready to serve.

Serves 8

Toffee Bar Cookies

1 cup butter or margarine	1 cup all-purpose flour
1 cup brown sugar	⅔ cup crushed nuts
1 egg yolk	6 milk chocolate candy bars

- Preheat oven to 350 degrees.
- Cream butter, sugar and egg yolk.
- Add flour gradually and blend.
- Mix nuts into batter.
- Spread in lightly greased 9x13-inch pan.
- Bake 20 minutes.
- Top with chocolate bars.
- Cool and cut in squares.

Yields 3 dozen

Aunt Lou's Ice Box Cookies

1½ cups shortening	2 teaspoons ground cinnamon
1 cup brown sugar	4 cups all-purpose flour
½ cup sugar	1 cup pecan pieces
3 medium eggs	1 cup chocolate chips
1 teaspoon baking soda	

- Cream shortening and sugars.
- Add eggs 1 at a time, beating well after each addition.
- Sift baking soda, cinnamon and flour into creamed mixture.
- Divide dough in half.
- Add nuts to one half and chocolate chips to other half.
- Form into log-shaped rolls.
- Wrap in foil; chill overnight.
- Preheat oven to 400 degrees.
- Slice into ¼-inch thickness.
- Bake for 5-8 minutes.

Yields 3 dozen

Chocolate Crinkle Cookies

½	cup corn oil	½	teaspoon salt
⅔	cup cocoa	2	cups sifted all-purpose flour
2	cups sugar		
4	eggs	2	teaspoons baking powder
2	teaspoons vanilla	1	cup confectioners' sugar

- Mix corn oil, cocoa and sugar with electric mixer.
- Blend in 1 egg at a time, until well mixed.
- Add vanilla.
- Stir in salt, flour and baking powder.
- Cover bowl with plastic wrap and chill several hours or overnight.
- Preheat oven to 350 degrees.
- Form dough by teaspoonfuls into 1-inch balls.
- Roll balls in confectioners' sugar and place 2 inches apart on greased baking sheet.
- Bake 8 minutes.

Yields 3 dozen

Coconut Oatmeal Cookies

1	cup butter or margarine	1	teaspoon vanilla
1	cup white sugar (heap a bit)	½	teaspoon salt
		1	can flaked coconut
1	cup brown sugar	2	cups oatmeal (quick-cooking)
2	medium eggs		
2	cups all-purpose flour	1	cup pecan pieces
1	teaspoon baking powder	1	cup butterscotch morsels (optional)
1	teaspoon baking soda		

- Preheat oven to 350 degrees.
- Cream butter and sugars.
- Add eggs and mix well.
- Add flour, baking powder, baking soda, vanilla and salt.
- Fold in coconut, oats, pecans and morsels by hand.
- Drop by teaspoonfuls onto ungreased cookie sheet.
- Bake for 10-12 minutes.

Yields 8 dozen

Coffee and Chocolate Pecan Squares

Crust

2¼ cups all-purpose flour　　　　**½　cup softened butter**
1　cup dark brown sugar　　　　　**1　cup chopped pecans**

- Preheat oven to 350 degrees.
- Blend flour, sugar and butter.
- Press into 13x9x2-inch glass baking dish.
- Sprinkle chopped pecans over crust.

Caramel Layer

⅔　cup butter　　　　　　　　　　　**½　cup dark brown sugar**

- Put butter and dark brown sugar in small saucepan.
- Cook over medium heat, stirring constantly, until mixture boils.
- Continue boiling 1 minute.
- Pour on top of crust.
- Bake 20 minutes.

Chocolate Layer

1　(6-ounce) package semi-　　　　**1　teaspoon coffee-flavored**
**　　sweet chocolate chips**　　　　　　**　liqueur**

- Sprinkle chocolate chips over caramel layer.
- Drizzle coffee-flavored liqueur over chocolate.
- When chocolate melts, swirl with knife.
- Cool and cut into squares.

Yields 3 dozen

Tuscany Biscotti

½ cup whole almonds	1 tablespoon grated orange zest
⅓ cup butter	
¾ cup sugar	2¼ cups all-purpose flour
2 eggs	1½ teaspoons baking powder
1 teaspoon vanilla extract	¼ teaspoon ground nutmeg
¼ teaspoon almond extract	¼ teaspoon salt

- Preheat oven to 325 degrees.
- Place almonds on a shallow pan and toast for 8-10 minutes, or until golden brown. Cool and cut into thirds. Reserve.
- Cream butter and sugar until light and fluffy.
- Beat in eggs, vanilla and almond extracts and orange zest.
- In separate bowl, combine flour, baking powder, nutmeg and salt.
- Add to creamed mixture, mixing until well blended.
- Stir in almonds.
- Divide dough in half. The dough will be soft, so keep your hands floured to handle dough.
- Grease baking sheet or cover with parchment paper. Shape dough into 2 logs on pan. Logs should be about 12 inches long, ½-inch wide and ½-inch thick. Space logs 2 inches apart.
- Bake for 25 minutes or until light golden brown.
- Carefully place on a cooling rack for 5 minutes.
- Place on a cutting surface. Using an electric knife or serrated knife, slice diagonally at 45 degrees about ½-inch thick.
- Arrange slices flat on baking sheet and return to oven for 5 minutes.
- Turn slices on opposite side and return to oven for 5 more minutes. Oven is still at 325 degrees.
- Cool on rack and store in tightly sealed container.

Yields 3½ dozen

Uses of an Electric Knife

- To horizontally split a cake layer
- To cut smaller pieces of bundt cake or layer cake
- To peel a grapefruit
- To peel a pineapple
- To shred lettuce in thin strips, as for tacos
- To remove crust from bread and cut tea sandwiches in sections
- And to slice turkey, tenderloin, ham or corned beef

Double Chocolate Cookies

4 ounces unsweetened,
   chopped chocolate
3 cups semi-sweet chocolate
   chips (divided in half)
½ cup butter, cut in pieces
½ cup all-purpose flour

½ teaspoon baking powder
½ teaspoon salt
4 large eggs
1½ cups sugar
1½ tablespoons instant coffee,
   dissolved in 2 teaspoons
   vanilla

- Preheat oven to 350 degrees.
- Melt unsweetened chocolate, ½ of semi-sweet chocolate chips and butter in microwave.
- Stir until smooth.
- Sift flour, baking powder and salt together in a separate bowl.
- Beat eggs and sugar with a mixer until light and thick.
- Fold in chocolate mixture, flour, remaining ½ of semi-sweet chocolate chips and vanilla coffee mixture.
- Let stand 15 minutes.
- Drop by tablespoonfuls on a baking sheet covered with parchment.
- Bake for 12 minutes (until puffed).
- Let stand 5 minutes and remove to racks to cool.

Yields 3 dozen

Date Chews

1 cup sugar
2 eggs
1 pound chopped dates

2 cups chopped pecans
¾ cup self-rising flour
1 teaspoon vanilla

- Preheat oven to 275 degrees.
- Mix sugar, eggs, dates, pecans, flour and vanilla.
- Drop on greased cookie sheet by tablespoonfuls.
- Bake for 30 minutes.
- Remove from cookie sheet and allow to cool on cooling rack.

Yields 3 dozen

Little Hands Sugar Cookies

1 cup margarine	2½ cups all-purpose flour
1½ cups confectioners' sugar	1 teaspoon baking soda
1 teaspoon vanilla	1 teaspoon cream of tartar
1 egg	

- Cream margarine and confectioners' sugar together.
- Add vanilla and egg and cream together.
- Add flour, baking soda and cream of tartar and stir into creamed mixture.
- Cover and place in refrigerator for 2-3 hours.
- Preheat oven to 375 degrees.
- Sprinkle confectioners' sugar on wax paper and roll out dough about ¼- to ⅜-inch thick.
- Cut with cookie cutter and place on ungreased cookie sheet.
- Bake for 10 minutes or until barely brown.
- Sprinkle with confectioners' sugar or regular sugar.

Yields 2 dozen

Cookie dough shaped into a roll and wrapped in parchment paper makes a wonderful presentation. Wrap the ends of the roll with ribbon or string. Attach baking instructions. Freeze, and you will have a handy, thoughtful gift for a new neighbor, busy mother or bachelor with a sweet tooth.

Chocolate Torte with Raspberry Yogurt Sauce

¾ cup unsalted butter
1⅓ cups sugar, divided
3 egg yolks
1⅓ cups milk
½ cup heavy cream
1 teaspoon vanilla sugar
6 ounces good quality chocolate

2 eggs
1 teaspoon baking powder
1½ cups cake flour
  pinch salt
  Marsala wine
  confectioners' sugar
  fresh raspberries

- Preheat oven to 325 degrees.
- Line bottom of a 9- or 9½-inch spring-form pan with parchment paper. Sprinkle parchment paper with a little cake flour after buttering it.
- Place butter and 1 cup of sugar in mixing bowl; beat until the butter loses its yellow color. Set aside.
- Make custard by combining the egg yolks, ⅓ cup of milk, the cream and vanilla in a double boiler and whisking until custard has thickened. Remove from heat and stir in chocolate and the remaining sugar. Let cool.
- Add eggs, 1 at a time, to the butter mixture, then add chocolate custard.
- Sift baking powder, cake flour and salt together and add to the mixture alternately with the remaining 1 cup of milk.
- Pour into prepared pan. Place pan in larger pan; add hot water to halfway up the side of the larger pan.
- Bake for 60-70 minutes. Cool on rack.
- Take a small cake tester and make a few small holes in the top of the cake. Pour a small amount of wine over the top to absorb in cake.
- Sprinkle with confectioners' sugar and garnish with fresh raspberries.

Serves 8

Vanilla Sugar

1 vanilla bean, cut into ½-inch pieces

1 cup sugar

- Grind vanilla in a blender until finely flaked.
- Add sugar and process until sugar mixture reaches a fine consistency.
- Store in a tightly sealed container.

Yields 1 cup

Raspberry Yogurt Sauce

1 cup low-fat vanilla yogurt	1 cup raspberry topping
1 cup frozen vanilla yogurt	

- Stir by hand both low-fat yogurt and frozen yogurt until they have a smooth consistency.
- Cover the bottom of each dessert plate with this mixture.
- Place raspberry topping in a squeeze bottle and dot sauce on outer edge of each plate. Place a slice of torte on each plate and drizzle with raspberry sauce.

Yields 2 cups

White Chocolate Cake

¼ pound white chocolate (white baking bar)	2½ cups all-purpose flour
½ cup boiling water	1 cup buttermilk
1½ cups softened butter, divided	1 cup coconut flakes
2 cups sugar	1 cup broken walnut or pecan pieces
4 eggs	1 box confectioners' sugar
2 teaspoons vanilla extract, divided	1 (8-ounce) package softened cream cheese
1 teaspoon baking soda	1 tablespoon milk

- Preheat oven to 350 degrees.
- Grease and flour a 9x13-inch baking pan. Set aside.
- Stir chocolate into boiling water until melted. Set aside to cool.
- Cream 1 cup butter and sugar until light.
- Add eggs, 1 at a time, mixing well after each.
- Add chocolate and 1 teaspoon vanilla and mix well.
- Add soda to flour, mixing well and add to butter mixture, alternating with the buttermilk.
- Stir in coconut and nuts and pour into prepared pan.
- Bake for 35-45 minutes.
- Cool before icing.
- Mix confectioners' sugar, cream cheese, milk, ½ cup butter and 1 teaspoon vanilla extract until smooth.
- Spread over cooled cake.

Serves 16

Green Apple Cake

1½ cups cooking oil
2 cups sugar
1 teaspoon vanilla
3 eggs
3 cups all-purpose flour
1 teaspoon baking soda
1 teaspoon salt

1 teaspoon cinnamon
3 cups chopped, raw green
  apples
1½ cups chopped pecans
½ cup margarine
1 cup brown sugar
¼ cup milk

• Preheat oven to 350 degrees.
• Mix together oil, white sugar, vanilla and eggs.
• Add flour, baking soda, salt and cinnamon.
• Fold in apples and pecans.
• Pour in well greased and floured tube pan.
• Bake for 1 hour or until done.
• Mix together margarine, brown sugar and milk.
• Cook topping for 3 minutes and pour over cake while hot.
• Let cake cool in pan.

Serves 16

Flourless Chocolate Cake

1 pound chopped, semi-
  sweet chocolate
1 cup sweet butter

2 tablespoons hazelnut
  liqueur
8 eggs, separated
1½ cups sugar

• Preheat oven to 350 degrees.
• Melt chocolate and butter in double boiler; cool to room temperature
  and add liqueur.
• Whip egg yolks and sugar until thick and pale.
• Whip egg whites until stiff.
• Fold ⅓ chocolate into yolks. Fold in ⅓ whites. Fold in rest of
  chocolate and whites.
• Butter and flour a 10-inch spring-form pan and pour in batter.
• Bake 25-30 minutes. Edges will be set, but not center.
• Cool in pan, then chill overnight.
• Serve with coffee or chocolate sauce or orange glaze. Top with
  whipped cream.

Serves 10

Coffee Sauce

½ cup sugar
½ cup water

1¾ tablespoons coffee-flavored
liqueur

- Combine sugar and water in small saucepan.
- Bring to a boil and stir until sugar is dissolved.
- Remove from heat. Stir in liqueur. Let cool completely.

Yields ½ cup

Chocolate Sauce

6 ounces chopped,
   bittersweet chocolate

¾ cup heavy cream

- Place chocolate in a small bowl.
- Scald cream in a saucepan over low heat.
- Pour over chocolate and let stand 5 minutes. Stir until smooth.
- Set over a pan of warm water until ready to use.

Yields 1 cup

Orange Glaze

¾ teaspoon unflavored
   gelatin
7 tablespoons orange juice

2¼ tablespoons sugar
¼ teaspoon cornstarch

- Sprinkle gelatin over 2 tablespoons orange juice. Let soften for
  10 minutes.
- Bring sugar and 4 tablespoons orange juice to a boil.
- Combine remaining juice and cornstarch in a small bowl. Dissolve and
  add to orange juice.
- Stir in gelatin and pour over cake.

Yields ½ cup

Possessed by Chocolate

4 squares baking chocolate	1 teaspoon baking powder
1½ cups margarine, divided	1 teaspoon baking soda
4¼ cups sugar, divided	1½ cups buttermilk
5 eggs	2 teaspoons vanilla, divided
3 cups sifted, all-purpose flour	⅓ cup cocoa
	⅓ cup white corn syrup
½ teaspoon salt	½ cup milk

- Preheat oven to 350 degrees.
- Melt chocolate in ceramic dish over boiling water.
- Cream 1 cup margarine and 2¼ cups sugar.
- Add eggs, 1 at a time, mixing well.
- Sift flour, salt, baking powder and baking soda together and add buttermilk, alternating dry and liquid ingredients.
- Add melted chocolate and 1 teaspoon vanilla.
- Pour into 4 greased and wax papered round cake pans.
- Bake about 15-20 minutes.
- Mix cocoa and remaining sugar. Add corn syrup and milk.
- Cook to soft-ball stage. Add remaining margarine and 1 teaspoon vanilla. Beat well.
- Cool and spread on cake.

Serves 12

Chocolate-Nut Cupcakes

⅔ cup cocoa (or 4 squares semi-sweet chocolate)	1¾ cups granulated sugar
1 cup margarine	1 cup unsifted, all-purpose flour
1½ cups broken pecans	2 teaspoons vanilla
4 large eggs	2 tablespoons vegetable oil

- Preheat oven to 325 degrees.
- Melt chocolate and margarine together.
- Add nuts and stir until well coated.
- Combine eggs, sugar, flour, vanilla and oil. Stir only until blended.
- Fold in chocolate-nut mixture.
- Fill foil muffin cups ⅔-full. Place in muffin tin.
- Bake for 20 minutes.

Yields 20 cupcakes

Frozen Chocolate Cheesecake

2 packages chocolate graham
   crackers, crushed
6 tablespoons melted butter
1 (8-ounce) package softened
   cream cheese
1 teaspoon vanilla
½ cup sugar, divided

1 (6-ounce) package semi-
   sweet chocolate chips
2 separated eggs
1 cup whipping cream,
   whipped
¾ cup chopped nuts

- Preheat oven to 325 degrees.
- Mix graham cracker crumbs and butter together. Press into an 8- or 9-inch spring-form pan.
- Bake for 10 minutes. Cool for about 1 hour.
- Beat together cream cheese, vanilla and ¼ cup sugar until well blended.
- Melt chocolate chips over low heat in heavy saucepan.
- Stir 2 beaten egg yolks and chocolate into cream cheese mixture. Mix well.
- Beat 2 egg whites until stiff peaks form; gradually add ¼ cup sugar. Beat until stiff.
- Fold into cream cheese mixture. Fold in the whipped whipping cream. Add nuts if desired.
- Pour into crust and freeze.
- May top with whipped cream before serving.
- May be made up to 3 days ahead.

Serves 10

Chocolate-Marble Praline Cheesecake

1½ cups graham cracker
    crumbs
¼ cup sugar
¼ cup melted butter
1¼ cups firmly packed brown
    sugar
2 tablespoons all-purpose
    flour

3 (8-ounce) packages
    softened cream cheese
3 beaten eggs
1½ teaspoons vanilla
1 square melted,
    unsweetened chocolate
½ cup pecan halves
1 (6-ounce) jar caramel
    topping

- Preheat oven to 350 degrees.
- Combine graham cracker crumbs, white sugar and melted butter. Press into bottom of ungreased 9-inch spring-form pan.
- Bake for 10-12 minutes. Remove from oven and cool.
- In small bowl, mix brown sugar and flour. Set aside.
- In large bowl, beat cream cheese with electric mixer while adding brown sugar mixture gradually. Add eggs and vanilla; beat only until incorporated.
- Measure out 1 cup of cream cheese mixture into small bowl and add chocolate.
- Pour large bowl of batter over graham cracker crust.
- Drop teaspoonfuls of chocolate over plain batter. Gently run knife through batters to marble.
- Arrange pecan halves around top edge of cheesecake.
- Bake for 45-55 minutes or until set.
- Remove from oven and loosen cake from sides of pan with knife or spatula.
- Cool completely, then refrigerate at least 2 hours.
- To serve, remove sides of pan. Spread caramel topping over top of cheesecake.
- Cut into slices and enjoy.

Serves 8-12

Pineapple Cheesecake

2 cups graham cracker crumbs	½ cup + 2 tablespoons sugar, divided
½ cup sugar	½ cup drained, crushed pineapple
½ cup melted butter	
2 (8-ounce) packages softened cream cheese	2 tablespoons flour
	2 teaspoons vanilla, divided
2 eggs	1 cup sour cream

- Preheat oven to 375 degrees.
- Mix crumbs, sugar and butter. Press into bottom and up sides of a 9-inch deep pie pan or spring-form pan.
- Cream cheese until smooth.
- Beat eggs slightly with ½ cup sugar, pineapple, flour and 1 teaspoon vanilla. Blend in cheese.
- Pour into crust and bake for 20 minutes. Remove from oven and let stand for 15 minutes.
- Combine sour cream, remaining 2 tablespoons sugar and 1 teaspoon vanilla. Spread on top of baked filling.
- Increase oven to 425 degrees and bake for 10 minutes.
- Cool. Chill overnight.

Serves 8-10

Grandmother's Caramel Icing

2 cups sugar	1 teaspoon baking soda
1 cup butter	1 teaspoon vanilla flavoring
1 cup buttermilk	

- Place sugar, butter, buttermilk, baking soda and vanilla flavoring in a heavy deep boiler.
- Cook until it reaches soft-ball stage.
- Remove from heat and cool.
- Cream with a large spoon until it is thick and looks like light caramel candy.

Will spread 3 layers

Nut-Rippled Spice Cake

¾ cup chopped pecans
½ cup firmly packed brown sugar
3 cups + 2 tablespoons all-purpose flour
2¼ teaspoons cinnamon, divided
2 tablespoons softened butter
3 teaspoons baking powder
½ teaspoon allspice
½ teaspoon nutmeg
1 teaspoon salt
1 cup sugar
⅔ cup firmly packed brown sugar
½ cup shortening
3 eggs
1 cup milk
1 teaspoon vanilla
1 cup sifted confectioners' sugar
3-4 tablespoons cream

- Preheat oven to 350 degrees.
- Combine pecans, ½ cup brown sugar, 2 tablespoons flour, 1 teaspoon cinnamon and softened butter. Reserve.
- Sift 3 cups flour, baking powder, 1 teaspoon cinnamon, allspice, nutmeg and salt. Set aside.
- Add sugar and ⅔ cup brown sugar to shortening gradually until well creamed.
- Add eggs to sugar mixture, 1 at a time, beating well after each.
- Combine milk and vanilla. Add alternately with dry ingredients to creamed mixture. Blend thoroughly.
- Spread ½ of batter in 13x9x2-inch, well greased and lightly floured pan. Sprinkle with all but ¼ cup of pecan mixture.
- Top with remaining batter. Sprinkle with remaining pecan mixture.
- Bake for 50-60 minutes.
- Blend confectioners' sugar, ¼ teaspoon cinnamon and cream to make a soft glaze.
- Drizzle over cake while still warm.

Serves 10-12

Banana Cake

1 cup softened margarine
2 cups sugar
2 eggs
2¾ cups all-purpose flour
1½ teaspoons baking powder
1 cup milk, divided
2 teaspoons baking soda

1½ cups mashed, very ripe bananas
1 (8-ounce) package softened cream cheese
1 pound confectioners' sugar
1 teaspoon vanilla
2 teaspoons milk
1 cup chopped pecans

- Preheat oven to 350 degrees.
- Cream margarine and sugar. Add eggs.
- Combine flour and baking powder. Then add flour alternately with ⅔ cup milk to creamed mixture.
- Stir baking soda into ⅓ cup milk and add bananas.
- Pour into 3 greased and floured 9-inch cake pans.
- Bake 25-30 minutes.
- Cool 15 minutes and turn onto wax paper. Cool completely.
- Mix cream cheese and confectioners' sugar. Add vanilla.
- Add 2 teaspoons milk to desired consistency. May need to add more than 2 teaspoons.
- Spread between layers and on sides and top.
- Sprinkle with pecans.
- Refrigerate after first 24 hours.

Serves 12

Butter-Roasted Pecans

1 cup pecans

⅓ cup melted butter

- Preheat oven to 300 degrees.
- Place pecans on baking sheet and drizzle with butter.
- Bake for 15 minutes.
- Cool and chop pecans.

Yields ½ cup

Caramel-Nut Pound Cake

1 cup butter	½ teaspoon salt
½ cup shortening	½ teaspoon baking powder
1 cup sugar	1 (5-ounce) can evaporated
1 box brown sugar	milk
5 large eggs	½ cup water
3 cups sifted, all-purpose	1 tablespoon vanilla
flour	1 cup chopped nuts

- Preheat oven to 325 degrees.
- Cream butter and shortening until fluffy.
- Add sugar and brown sugar 1 cup at a time.
- Add eggs 1 at a time.
- Sift flour, salt and baking powder together.
- Add to creamed mixture alternately with evaporated milk and water. Add vanilla and nuts.
- Pour into greased and floured tube pan.
- Bake for 1½ hours.
- Cake can be frosted or served plain.

Frosting

¼ cup butter or margarine	1 cup chopped, butter-roasted
2 cups sifted confectioners'	pecans (recipe on page 207)
sugar	1 teaspoon vanilla
	¼-½ cup milk

- Cream butter and confectioners' sugar and add butter-roasted pecans.
- Add vanilla and enough milk for the consistency desired.
- Spread over warm cake.

Serves 16

Kentucky Pound Cake

6 large eggs
2⅔ cups sugar
2 cups butter at room
   temperature

3½ cups cake flour
8 tablespoons half-and-half
   cream
1 teaspoon vanilla

- Preheat oven to 300 degrees.
- Use a heavy duty stand mixer.
- Separate eggs. Beat whites and add 6 level tablespoons of sugar after eggs hold peaks. Place in refrigerator.
- Cream butter, add rest of the sugar and beat until light.
- Add eggs yolks, 2 at a time, beating well after each.
- Add flour and cream alternately. Beat mixture until light, about 10 minutes.
- Fold in egg whites. Add vanilla.
- Pour batter into a greased bundt pan.
- Bake 1½ hours or until cake tester comes out clean.

Serves 16

Lemon Buttermilk Pound Cake

1½ cups butter or margarine
3 cups sugar, divided
4 eggs
3½ cups cake flour
½ teaspoon salt

½ teaspoon baking soda
1 cup buttermilk
1 teaspoon lemon extract
   juice of 2 large lemons

- Preheat oven to 325 degrees.
- Cream butter and 2½ cups sugar. Add eggs 1 at a time.
- In separate bowl, mix flour, salt and baking soda.
- Add dry ingredients alternately with buttermilk to creamed mixture. Beat well.
- Add lemon extract.
- Bake in greased and floured tube pan for 1 hour and 15 minutes.
- Mix remaining ½ cup sugar and lemon juice. Heat until sugar dissolves.
- Make holes in warm cake with skewer to allow topping to penetrate cake.

Serves 16

Pineapple Pound Cake

½ cup shortening	1 teaspoon vanilla
1 cup butter	¾ cup crushed pineapple,
2¾ cups sugar	undrained
6 eggs	¼ cup melted butter
3 cups all-purpose flour	1½ cups confectioners' sugar
1 teaspoon baking powder	1 cup crushed pineapple,
¼ cup milk	drained

- Combine shortening, butter and sugar. Cream until light and fluffy.
- Add eggs, 1 at a time. Combine flour and baking powder. Add to cream mixture, alternating with milk and vanilla, beating well after each addition.
- Stir in ¾ cup crushed pineapple.
- Pour batter into a greased and floured 10-inch tube pan.
- Place in cold oven. Set temperature at 325 degrees; bake 1 hour and 15 minutes until done. Cool 10-15 minutes in pan.
- Invert onto serving plate.
- Combine melted butter and confectioners' sugar until smooth. Stir in drained pineapple.
- Drizzle glaze over top and sides.

Serves 16

Our League members submitted many great recipes for the much-anticipated pound cake contest. After a serious and guilt-free morning of tasting and testing each and every recipe, we awarded this Pineapple Pound Cake with our First Prize.

Refrigerator Fruit Cake

1½ cups margarine
1   pound marshmallows
1   pound crushed graham
    crackers
1   pound shelled pecans
    (4 cups)
4   tablespoons brown sugar

2   teaspoons vanilla extract
2   (8-ounce) boxes pitted
    dates
½   pound candied cherries
¼   pound citron, cut fine
¼   pound chopped, candied
    pineapple

- In top of double boiler, melt margarine and marshmallows.
- Put crushed graham crackers, pecans, brown sugar and vanilla in a large bowl. Add dates, cherries, citron and pineapple.
- Add marshmallow and butter mixture and mix well.
- Mold or shape into roll.
- Wrap in wax paper and store in refrigerator.
- Cut into slices to serve.

Serves 16

Lemon Pineapple Cake

3   cups cake flour
1   teaspoon salt
1   teaspoon baking powder
½   cup shortening
1   cup + 1 tablespoon butter
3¾ cups sugar
5   eggs

1   teaspoon vanilla
1   cup milk
1   cup crushed pineapple,
    drained
2   egg yolks
    juice of ½ lemon
3   tablespoons flour

- Preheat oven to 325 degrees.
- Sift flour, salt and baking powder together.
- In separate bowl, cream shortening, 1 cup butter and 3 cups sugar. Add eggs, 1 at a time. Add vanilla.
- Alternately add dry ingredients and milk to sugar mixture.
- Bake in 4 layers until brown. Test with toothpick for doneness.
- Cook pineapple, ¾ cup sugar, 1 tablespoon butter, egg yolks, lemon juice and flour until thick enough to spread.
- Spread between cake layers.
- Frost with 7-minute frosting or other white frosting.

Serves 12

Fresh Peach Cake

¼ cup softened butter	¾ cup milk
1 cup sugar	1½ cups thinly sliced, fresh
2 eggs	peaches
1¾ teaspoons almond extract,	2 tablespoons lemon juice
divided	½ cup butter
1¾ cups all-purpose flour	¾ cup brown sugar
2 teaspoons baking powder	½ cup flaked coconut
½ teaspoon salt	2 tablespoons half-and-half

- Preheat oven to 350 degrees.
- In a mixer, cream ¼ cup butter and white sugar until light.
- Add eggs 1 at a time, beating well. Add ¾ teaspoon almond extract and beat well.
- Combine flour, baking powder and salt in separate bowl. Add creamed mixture alternately with milk. Mix well.
- Pour into greased 9x9-inch baking pan. Bake for 30 minutes. Cool cake in pan for 10 minutes.
- Combine peaches and lemon juice. Stir to coat. Drain fruit.
- Arrange peaches on top of cake.
- Melt ½ cup butter in small pan. Add brown sugar, coconut, half-and-half and 1 teaspoon almond extract.
- Mix well and pour over peaches evenly. Broil 2 minutes or until bubbly and light brown.
- Cool slightly and cut into squares.

Serves 6-10

Sugar "Shell"

Pumpkin Cream Roll

3 eggs	1 cup chopped nuts
1 cup sugar	confectioners' sugar
⅔ cup canned pumpkin	1 (8-ounce) package cream
1 teaspoon lemon juice	cheese
¾ cup all-purpose flour	¼ cup butter
1 teaspoon baking powder	1 cup confectioners' sugar
2 teaspoons pumpkin pie	1 teaspoon vanilla
spice	

- Preheat oven to 375 degrees.
- Beat eggs in medium bowl. Gradually beat in sugar.
- Fold in pumpkin and lemon juice.
- Fold in flour, baking powder and pumpkin pie spice.
- Pour into a well greased 10x15-inch pan. Sprinkle with nuts.
- Bake for 15 minutes.
- Quickly loosen sides with knife. Turn onto thin towel generously sprinkled with powdered sugar.
- Roll up in towel and cool thoroughly.
- Combine cream cheese, butter, confectioners' sugar and vanilla.
- Unroll cake, spread filling and roll up again.
- Wrap in foil and chill.
- Slice and serve.

Serves 8

Date Orange Cake

1 cup margarine or butter	1 teaspoon baking soda
2¾ cups sugar, divided	½ teaspoon salt
4 eggs	1⅓ cups buttermilk
1 teaspoon vanilla	1½ cups chopped dates
3 tablespoons grated orange rind, divided	1½ cups pecans, coarsely chopped
4 cups all-purpose flour, divided	½ cup orange juice

- Preheat oven to 350 degrees.
- Cream butter and 2 cups sugar.
- Beat in eggs, 1 at a time. Add vanilla and 2 tablespoons orange rind.
- Sift 3½ cups flour with soda and salt.
- Add alternately with buttermilk to the butter mixture.
- Mix dates and pecans with ½ cup flour. Add to batter.
- Pour into a greased and floured bundt or tube pan.
- Bake for 1 hour and 15 minutes.
- Blend ¾ cup sugar, orange juice and 1 tablespoon orange rind.
- Pour glaze over cake while still in pan and while cake is warm.

Serves 16

Music is the finishing touch for a festive affair. Always work within your budget, keeping your guests in mind. Decide if you want music in the background or as the center of attention, allowing it to assist you in successfully composing your special occasion.

Eloquence

Extras

Eloquence
Lunt Silversmiths
Greenfield, Massachusetts

Eloquence, introduced in 1953, was designed by Nord Bowlen, son of William C. Bowlen, one of the three original owners of the company (Rogers, Lunt and Bowlen). The design, which combines Rococo elements (scrolls, flowers and leaves) in a waisted terminal, recalls 18th Century France. This traditional design bucked the trend of the 1950's, favoring a more modern, simpler and often asymmetric style. It nevertheless became, and remains, quite popular.

The Lunt organization shares its family tree with Towle Silversmiths (q.v.). When the A. F. Towle Company failed in 1900, it was purchased by George Lunt, who was joined by Rogers and Bowlen to form Rogers, Lunt and Bowlen in 1902. Since 1935, the company has used the tradename Lunt Silversmiths. The firm is still family-operated. A few years ago, when Tiffany & Company decided to stop making their own flatware, they chose Lunt to produce it for them.

Pictured: Grape shears, English napkin ring, Eloquence place setting, individual salt cellar with spoon and Warwick flow blue plate by Johnson Bros., circa 1900

Warek Eenab
(Stuffed Grape Leaves)

1 **cup rice**	2 **tablespoons melted butter**
20 **grape leaves,**	¼ **teaspoon cinnamon**
approximately	1 **teaspoon salt**
1 **pound cooked, finely diced,**	**pepper to taste**
lean lamb or beef	¼ **cup lemon juice**

- Soak rice 10 minutes in water.
- Line the bottom of a large cooking pot with 2 or 3 layers of grape leaves.
- Drain rice and mix with meat, butter, cinnamon, salt and pepper.
- Roll about 1 tablespoon of meat mixture in a grape leaf using back of leaf. Turn in corners and form a meat roll. Place side by side in pan. Repeat with all leaves.
- Add water to cover rolls by ¼ inch. Invert a heat-proof plate over rolls to hold them down.
- Cover and simmer until rice is cooked, approximately 20-30 minutes.
- Add lemon juice and simmer another 5 minutes.

Serves 4

Lebanese food is an experience of the senses. These unique dishes are a pleasure to look at; the aroma is delightful and it prepares you for the magnificent taste. The Lebanese food is inspired by many different spices, which can enhance the recipe. Each recipe is unique, even though it may be of the same basic dish, simply because of that person's or family's palate.

There are few written recipes because it is the older women who pass down these recipes and traditional techniques. My husband's mother passed down their traditions to me. Many less-than-perfect dishes accrued in the beginning, until I learned the secrets of each recipe. I now look forward to passing this heritage down to my family.

–Karen Saliba

Tabbouleh

1	cup finely ground borghul (cracked wheat)	10	minced spinach leaves
1	finely diced cucumber	½	cup freshly squeezed lemon juice
2	finely diced tomatoes	¼	cup olive oil
1	minced, medium onion	1	tablespoon salt
10	minced springs of parsley		pepper to taste
1	finely diced green pepper	1	tablespoon pulverized mint leaves
10	finely chopped radishes		

- Wash borghul 2 or 3 times. Soak for 1 hour. Drain and squeeze moisture from borghul.
- Add cucumber, tomatoes, onion, parsley, green pepper, radishes and spinach, and mix well.
- Add lemon juice and olive oil along with salt and pepper.
- Garnish with mint.

Serves 6-8

Stuffed Cabbage

3	pounds lean ground beef	3	heads cabbage
	salt and pepper to taste	3	(15-ounce) cans tomato sauce
½	teaspoon seasoning salt		
1	teaspoon Worcestershire sauce	3	tablespoons fresh lemon juice
½	medium, grated onion	1½	cups brown sugar

- In large Dutch oven, brown ground beef. Add salt, pepper, seasoning salt, Worcestershire sauce and onion.
- Drain and reserve.
- Steam cabbage until leaves are soft and pliable. Divide leaves and fill with meat mixture. Secure with toothpick.
- Using same Dutch oven, prepare sauce by adding tomato sauce, lemon juice and brown sugar. Mix well.
- Place stuffed cabbage leaves in Dutch oven. Gently spoon sauce to cover.
- Cook slowly over low heat for 2 hours.

Yields approximately 30 cabbage rolls

Noodle Kugel

½	pound wide noodles	8	ounces regular cottage cheese
¾	cup butter	½	teaspoon salt
1	(8-ounce) package softened cream cheese	¾	cup sugar
3	eggs	2	teaspoons vanilla
2	cups sour cream	8	ounces warm milk

- Preheat oven to 350 degrees.
- Cook and drain noodles. Add butter immediately.
- Blend cream cheese, eggs, sour cream, cottage cheese, salt, sugar, vanilla and milk.
- Add to noodles.
- Pour into a glass baking dish and bake for 1 hour covered.
- Uncover, reduce heat to 300 degrees and bake an additional ½ hour.

Serves 8-10

This Noodle Kugel recipe was given to me by my sister-in-law, Helen Lifland, after using it for her sons' Bar Mitzvah celebrations. In keeping with tradition, I, too, have served it for my son's Bar Mitzvah and both of my daughters' Bat Mitzvah luncheons.

–Susan Blumberg

These recipes have become family favorites and are served at Jewish Holiday meals throughout the year. We hope that they become your favorites, too!

–Marilyn Granger

Mahmool

3 cups coarsely chopped walnuts or pecans	1 large box cream of wheat
1½ cups granulated sugar	1 tablespoon vanilla
1 teaspoon cinnamon	2 tablespoons flour
½ pound butter	1 cup milk
	½ cup confectioners' sugar

- Mix nuts, granulated sugar and cinnamon. Reserve.
- Cream butter and cream of wheat.
- Add vanilla; knead flour and milk into dough until dough is smooth.
- Roll dough out and cut into 3-inch circles.
- Place 1 tablespoon of nut mixture on each circle.
- Bake 25-30 minutes. Cakes will be light brown.
- Sprinkle with confectioners' sugar while hot.

Yields approximately 3 dozen

Ice Cream Strudel

1 cup softened butter	1 tablespoon cinnamon
1 cup melted vanilla ice cream	½ cup chopped pecans
	1 cup white raisins
2 cups all-purpose flour	1 cup coconut
1 cup sugar	18 ounces apricot preserves

- To make dough mixture, combine butter, ice cream and flour.
- Mix until well blended and stiff dough is formed.
- Separate dough into 3 balls and refrigerate overnight.
- Preheat oven to 350 degrees.
- Using well floured hands and rolling pin, roll stiff dough on wax paper into rectangle.
- Combine sugar and cinnamon.
- Combine pecans, raisins and coconut in separate bowl.
- Spread 6 ounces of preserves over dough, leaving ½ inch around sides without preserves.
- Sprinkle with ⅓ of coconut mixture, and then sprinkle with ⅓ of cinnamon sugar mixture.
- Using wax paper, roll dough jelly-roll-style with center seam on top.
- Tuck sides under and pinch closed. Repeat with other 2 dough balls.
- Bake on lightly greased pan for 45 minutes.
- Refrigerate before cutting.
- To serve, cut on diagonal with wet serrated knife. Freezes well.

Yields 36 slices

Special Occasion Schedule

Here are some guidelines to assist you in hosting that perfect special occasion:

Coffee   10:00 a.m. to 12:00 noon

Brunch   10:30 a.m. to 1:00 p.m.

Luncheon   Begins between 12:00 noon and 1:00 p.m. and lasts 1½-2 hours

Tea   Begins between 4:00 and 4:30 p.m. and ends promptly at 5:30 p.m.

Cocktail Party   Begins between 6:00 and 8:00 p.m. and lasts 45 minutes to an hour

Dinner   Begins between 8:00 and 9:00 p.m. and lasts 3-3½ hours (Cocktails may be served between 7:00 and 7:30 p.m.)

Coffee in Quantity

Servings	Coffee	Water
25	½ pound	1¼-1½ gallons
50	1 pound	2½-3 gallons
75	1½ pounds	3¾-4½ gallons
100	2 pounds	5-6 gallons

Keep coffee maker clean and free of residue. Start with freshly ground beans and cold water. Remove grounds as soon as brewing is completed. Serve immediately. Keep unused portion warm and do not serve after 1 hour. Do not reheat.

Setting up a coffee bar is a simple way to informally enjoy coffee. Freshly whipped cream, cinnamon sticks, chocolate chips or liqueurs are just a few items you may want to include. Consider the time of day you will be entertaining, as well as your menu and the personal taste of your invited guests.

Iced Tea in Quantity

Servings Over Ice	Tea	Boiling Water	Tap Water
25	¼ cup	2 gallons	1 gallon
50	½ cup	3 gallons	1½ gallons
75	1½ cups	4 gallons	2 gallons
100	2 cups	5 gallons	2½ gallons

Place tea leaves in a piece of cheesecloth and tie with kitchen twine. Pour boiling water over tea and allow to steep for 10-20 minutes. Remove cheesecloth bag and add tap water. Sweeten while tea is hot. You may choose to sweeten with simple syrup or other beverages, such as homemade lemonade.

Simple Syrup

1 cup granulated sugar   **1 cup water**

In heavy saucepan, combine sugar and water. Slowly bring to a boil. Stir to dissolve sugar. Simmer on low heat until mixture is clear. Remove from heat and cool before using.

Hot Tea in Quantity

6-ounce Servings	Loose Tea	Boiling Water
25	6-7 tablespoons	1¼ gallons
50	¾-1 cup	2½ gallons
75	1¼-1½ cups	3¾ gallons
100	2 cups	5 gallons

Place tea leaves on piece of cheesecloth and tie with kitchen twine or use a tea strainer. Pour hot water over tea and allow to steep for about 10 minutes. Larger volumes may take longer. Remove cheesecloth bag prior to serving.

When pouring hot tea into a china cup, place teaspoon in cup before pouring. Pour tea over spoon to avoid cracking the cup.

Menu Suggestions

Seated Dinner for Eight

Salmon-Stuffed Snow Peas
Mushroom Bisque
Asparagus with Basil Mayonnaise Sauce
Marinated Eye of Round Roast
Oven-Roasted Plum Tomatoes
Company's Coming Rice
Yeast Rolls
Almond-Stuffed Apples

Silver Anniversary Celebration for 50-75

Coffee Punch   Fall Punch
Pecan-Glazed Brie
Pesto Pasta Rolls
Mustard Shrimp Tortellini
Spicy Beef Bites
Bacon and Tomato Cocktail Rounds
Pineapple Pound Cake
Chocolate Crinkle Cookies
Coffee and Chocolate Pecan Squares
White Chocolate Cake
Mixed Nuts

Entertaining the Boss

Crabmeat Pâté
Artichoke Cream Soup
Châteaubriand with Cognac-Mustard Sauce
Lemon-Horseradish New Potatoes
Creamy Spinach Casserole
Carrots Vicky
Frozen Soufflé with Hot Strawberry Sauce

Light Spring Dinner

Mushroom Pinwheels
Salad Niçoise
Break Away Bread
Fresh Peach Cake

- Eloquence Extras -
Easy Brunch for Four
Tomato Citrus Consommé
Black Bean Salad
Ham and Fruit Roll-Ups
Grandmother's Cinnamon Rolls
Pralines and Cream

Weeknight Dinner
Fruit Salad with Blueberry Dressing
Beef Broccoli Wellington
Buttermilk Custard Pie

Salad Luncheon
Avocado and Tomato Aspic
New Potato Salad
Shrimp Vermicelli Salad
Spinach Poppy Seed Salad
Williamsburg Orange Muffins
Zucchini Nut Bread
Peachy Raspberry Sherbet

Family Mexican Night
Ensenada Salsa and Tortilla Chips
Congealed Fresh Vegetable Salad
Chicken Enchiladas
El Paso Pilaf
Foolproof Flan

Taste of the Tropics
St. Thomas Fruit Soup
Vidalia Onion Tart
Palm Artichoke Salad
Banana Nut Bread

Casual South of the Border Dinner

Mexican Pinwheels
Salad Radicchio
Winter White Chili
Jalapeño Cornbread
Coffee and Chocolate Pecan Squares

Sunday Night Dinner

Hot and Spicy Baked Italian Appetizer
Cold Marinated Beef Salad
English Muffin Loaf
Bourbon Ice Cream Parfait

Elegant Seafood Dinner

Phyllo Spinach and Cheese Bundles
York's Salad with Feta
Soft Shell Crab à la Toulouse
Garlic Mashed Potatoes
Herb Bread
Pineapple Cheesecake

Dinner on the Patio

Asparagus Roll-Ups
Fresh Tomato Salad
Tortellini and Shrimp
Savory Green Beans
Herb-Onion Rolls
Chocolate Torte with Raspberry Yogurt Sauce

Extra Special Saturday Lunch

Onion, Potato, and Roquefort Soup
Mandarin Orange Salad
Sausage Bread
Toffee Bar Cookies

Buffets

In order to serve a small group or a large crowd with little assistance, you may choose to serve a buffet. Careful planning is the key to success. Be sure to take into account the number of guests, menu, traffic patterns, beverages, seating, clearing stations and cleaning.

You must first determine the number of guests that can be conveniently served in the location chosen for your function. Then decide whether the buffet will be seated or standing and make all other decisions based on this information. For example, a seated buffet is your only option for foods that require using a knife, and all items must be served on one plate if you are expecting a large number of guests. Each dish of your buffet should be accompanied by a serving utensil and portions should be offered in individual servings. Avoid messy foods.

Give special consideration to the traffic pattern created by your buffet arrangement. Move furniture, if necessary, and set up several serving and clearing stations to accommodate large groups. If you need more space, move outside, but make alternate plans in case of inclement weather. To keep the traffic flowing, always serve your beverages in an area away from the food.

Take the extra time needed to adequately plan for every aspect of your buffet. The following illustrations will assist you with the planning.

Seated Buffet from a Sideboard

Place your glasses, napkins, silver flatware, bread and condiments on the dining table. When your guests have finished their dinner and the dishes are ready to be cleared, you may replace the dinner buffet with a dessert buffet. Coffee and other beverages should be placed on a smaller table and served by the host/hostess.

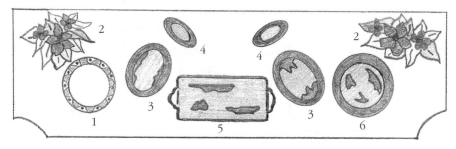

1. Dinner plates   **4.** Sauce or accompaniments
2. Flowers   **5.** Entrée
3. Side dishes   **6.** Additional food

Dessert Buffet from a Sideboard

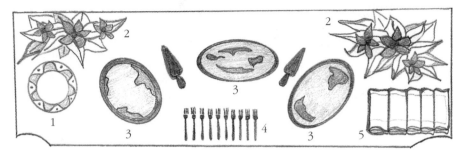

1. Dessert plates
2. Flowers or candles
3. Dessert selections
4. Dessert flatware
5. Napkins

Central Buffet

Serve this buffet from the dining table and begin at a point on the table nearest the entrance and exit of the room. If it is convenient, you may also choose to serve dessert and coffee from this table, or you can place them in another room to allow for clearing the buffet. Flatware may be placed at either the end or the beginning of the table, depending on preference. Always leave extra space between the serving dishes to allow your guests to set their plates down while serving.

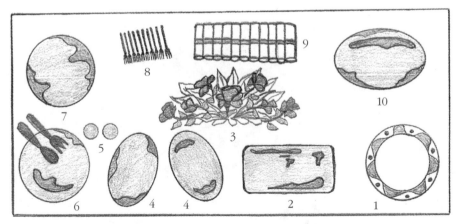

1. Dinner plates
2. Entrée
3. Centerpiece
4. Side dishes
5. Salt and pepper
6. Salad and dressings
7. Bread
8. Flatware
9. Napkins
10. Dessert

Parallel Buffet

To accommodate larger groups, set up a parallel buffet on the dining table and serve coffee and desserts in another room. This buffet only works if the entrance and exit are at opposite ends of the room. Serve each side of the table as follows:

1. Dinner plates
2. Entrée
3. Side dishes
4. Salt and pepper

5. Bread
6. Salad and dressing
7. Flatware and napkins

Circular Buffet

A buffet served from a round table is recommended for smaller groups. To avoid congestion, you need to serve beverages and desserts from a different area.

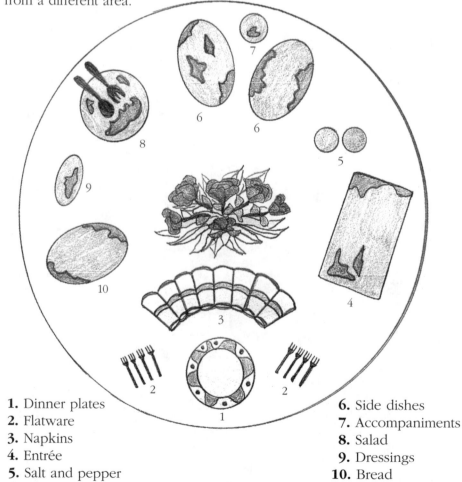

1. Dinner plates
2. Flatware
3. Napkins
4. Entrée
5. Salt and pepper

6. Side dishes
7. Accompaniments
8. Salad
9. Dressings
10. Bread

Table Settings

Strict etiquette once dictated the placement of all silver, china, crystal and linen. The rules are not as rigid today, but the basics still apply. The illustrations on the following pages are set forth as your guideline for a formal place setting and the sequence of a four course meal. Both formal table settings are correct and can be used according to preference.

Exceptions and cutlery substitutions may vary, but always follow the basic rules. Forks should be placed to the left, and spoons and knives to the right, with handles placed one inch from the edge of the table. The only exception to the rule is the cocktail or small fish fork, which is placed to the right with knives and spoons.

Silver flatware is always placed in order of service and should be worked from the outside in toward the plate. The first silver to be used is placed farthest from the plate on each side, and the last pieces to be used are closest to the plate. These are usually the dessert fork and spoon, unless they are placed horizontally above the dinner plate. When appropriate, you may replace the dessert spoon with a fruit knife.

You can place flatware, tines and bowls up or down, but be consistent with all placements. Knife blades should always face the dinner plate, and butter knives should be placed horizontally across the top of the bread plate, with blade down and handle right. You should not place more than three pieces of silver on either side of the plate at any time. If additional flatware is required for the meal, it should be brought with the course.

Unless dinner is to be served from a sideboard, serving pieces should be placed in the center of the table, nose to tail, next to the appropriate dish. The bread plate is placed to the left and above the forks, in alignment with the water glass, and the salad or service plate is placed on the dinner plate and removed after use. Folded napkins can be placed to the left, right, center, above or on the plate, as well as in a glass.

Water and wine glasses should be placed to the right of the dinner plate, above the knife, with the first glass to be used the closest. Wine should be poured with the appropriate course and the glasses removed afterwards. You should never have more than three glasses per table setting.

It is customary to serve coffee somewhere other than the table. But if you must, cups and saucers should be brought during or after dessert and placed to the right of your guests with a spoon on the saucer.

Your guests should be served from the left and plates removed from the right. Rules also dictate that beverages be served from the right.

Do not let these guidelines make entertaining an unpleasant experience. Instead, let them enhance your own practical rules and help you learn to enjoy hosting a dinner party.

Formal Place Setting

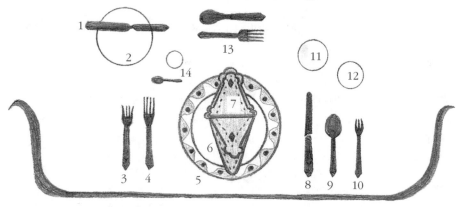

1. Butter knife	**8.** Dinner knife
2. Bread plate	**9.** Dinner spoon
3. Salad fork	**10.** Cocktail or fish fork
4. Dinner fork	**11.** Water glass
5. Dinner plate	**12.** Wine glass
6. Salad or service plate	**13.** Dessert spoon and fork
7. Napkin	**14.** Salt cellar and spoon

or

Formal Place Setting

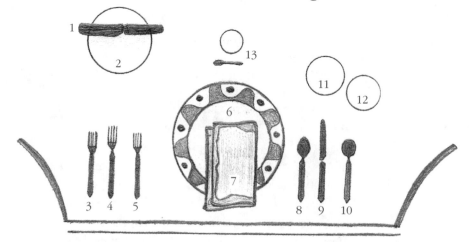

1. Butter knife	**8.** Dessert spoon
2. Bread plate	**9.** Dinner knife
3. Salad fork	**10.** Soup spoon
4. Dinner fork	**11.** Water glass
5. Dessert fork	**12.** Wine glass
6. Dinner plate	**13.** Salt cellar and spoon
7. Napkin	

Sequence of a Four Course Meal

Appetizer Course

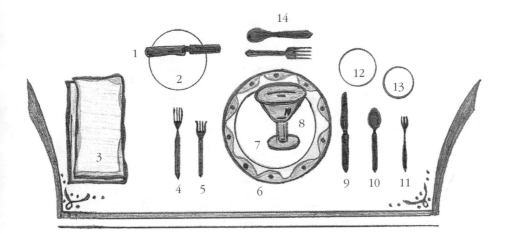

1. Butter knife (blade down, handle right)
2. Bread plate
3. Napkin
4. Dinner fork
5. Salad fork (placed right of dinner fork indicates salad will be served with or after main course; placed left of dinner fork indicates salad will be served before main course)
6. Dinner plate
7. Service plate (removed after appetizer course)
8. Appetizer dish
9. Dinner knife
10. Dinner spoon
11. Cocktail or fish fork
12. Water glass
13. Wine glass
14. Dessert spoon and fork (spoon top, handle right; fork bottom, handle left)

Soup Course

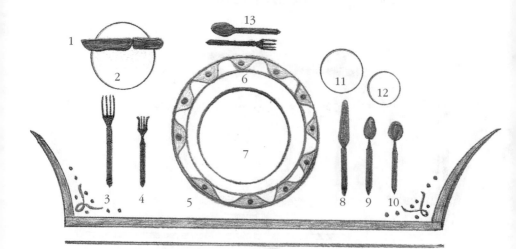

1. **Butter knife** (blade down, handle right)
2. **Bread plate**
3. **Dinner fork**
4. **Salad fork** (placed right of dinner fork indicates salad will be served with or after main course; placed left of dinner fork indicates salad will be served before main course)
5. **Dinner plate**
6. **Soup plate** (removed after soup course)
7. **Soup saucer** (removed after soup course)
8. **Dinner knife**
9. **Dinner spoon**
10. **Soup spoon** (removed after soup course)
11. **Water glass**
12. **Wine glass**
13. **Dessert spoon and fork** (spoon top, handle right; fork bottom, handle left)

Entrée or Main Course

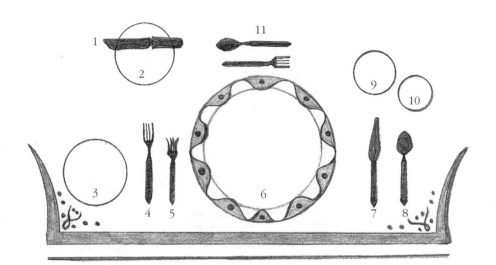

1. Butter knife (blade down, handle right)
2. Bread plate
3. Salad plate
4. Dinner fork
5. Salad fork (placed right of dinner fork indicates salad will be served with or after main course; placed left of dinner fork indicates salad will be served before main course)
6. Dinner plate
7. Dinner knife
8. Dinner spoon
9. Water glass
10. Wine glass
11. Dessert spoon and fork (spoon top, handle right; fork bottom, handle left)

Dessert Course

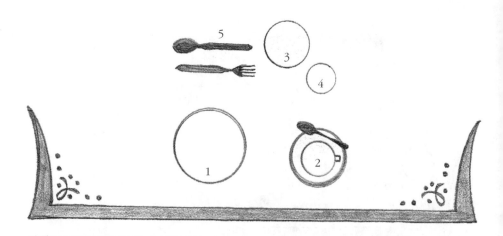

1. Dessert plate
2. Coffee cup and saucer with spoon
3. Water glass
4. Dessert wine (if served)
5. Dessert spoon and fork (spoon top, handle right; fork bottom, handle left)

Use and Care of Linens

Throughout history, the purpose of linens has tended to be both functional and decorative. For example, linen can be used to hide a marred table finish or to protect and enhance a beautiful one.

As your guideline when decorating for formal occasions, use damask for dinner, lighter linens for luncheons and organdies and laces for teas and coffees.

Consider the purchase of fine linens an investment in which the durability offsets the cost. Buy only those old linen table, bath, bed and window linens that are in good condition. Avoid those with rust spots because the spots usually become holes when efforts are made to remove them. If you find a damaged piece of lace, etc., that you love, be inventive. Place books, flowers, photos, plates and other accessories over flaws and enjoy.

In caring for your investment, remember that proper care is essential for long life. For new, 100 percent linens, follow the manufacturer's directions for care. But for old, linen linens, follow ours.

Linens should be dealt with immediately when soiled. If your cloth is solid – no lace, etc. – spray with a commercial remover, then soak in cold water, not hot which can set stains, in washing machine overnight. Spin out water on gentle cycle, add a pure liquid soap and wash in cold water on gentle cycle. Rinse thoroughly, at least three times, because soap and starch residue cause yellow spots on stored linens; drain and place in a clean, white plastic bag and freeze – yes freeze – until you are in the mood to iron. Take linens from freezer; thaw in bag to keep moisture even, then iron on the highest setting until dry. Remember, no starch!

The freezing takes out just the right amount of moisture so that your linens will actually look and feel starched. You may leave in freezer for weeks before ironing, with no harm done, but iron on the same day you thaw or your linens might mildew. After ironing dry, hang linen over a towel-covered shower rod, or any dowel, for several hours to be sure it is completely dry. A padded coat hanger works for napkins, placemats, handkerchiefs, etc.

Roll large linens over cardboard dowels from the fabric retailer and store upright. For long-term storage, cover cardboard with acid-free paper. If you must fold your linens, place light blue tissue paper between layers to protect and prevent yellowing.

Candle drips should be removed prior to washing. Scrape off as much wax as possible with a dull knife, then place layers of paper towel both over and under the spots while ironing with a warm iron until towels are clean. For small pieces, such as placemats, you might have success with holding over the sink and pouring boiling water over the wax.

Fragile linens or lace should be handled with care. If your piece is all lace, cutwork, insertion or delicate embroidery, wash as follows: Place a sheet in bottom of bathtub. Gently spread the item on the sheet, and pat soiled spots with capfuls of gentle, liquid laundry soap. Turn shower nozzle on cool, gentle spray and gently press item with hands until water runs completely clear. Leave item in tub until all water has dripped out, then gently gather item into a clean towel or towels and knead softly to remove remaining water. Now spread item out on a flat surface lined with plastic, such as a painter's drop cloth, to dry. An electric fan helps speed the process. Important: Never let a wet, fragile piece of linen "dangle" because the weight of the water might cause it to tear. That is why you always gather linen up when handling.

If a spot remains on your laundered piece, pour freshly-squeezed, drained lemon juice on the spot and place linen in a sunny window just until spot is gone. Then rinse only the spot area with cool water, dry, touch up with warm iron if needed and store. Your lace and fine cutwork should not need ironing because they are vulnerable to tears by the iron.

For crewel work, needlepoint, etc., rub soiled spot with a bar of octagon soap and gently rub between hands until stain is gone. Then rinse the spot thoroughly with cold water because hot water will shrink wool thread and sometimes change the color of and shrink your linens. Be careful to rub softly as wool thread is fragile. Then dry the spot and iron on the wrong side with warm setting if needed. Place a towel between ironing board and linen.

To freshen old quilts, select a warm, sunny day when the grass is green, and spread quilt directly on grass and leave all day. Given proper care, your linens will become more beautiful with age.

Linens add a polish to each and every occasion. Do not limit your use of them to only large, formal gatherings. Breakfast for two, soup in front of the fire and iced beverages on the patio are also the perfect occasions to enjoy fine things.

- *Eloquence Extras* -

Napkin Folds

One of the simplest ways to add a decorative touch to your special occasion is to fold the napkins in ingenious ways. Many folds are very simple, while others require a little dexterity.

We suggest that you always experiment with the folds prior to your function, selecting the fold most suitable to your occasion and table decor. Fold all napkins two to three days in advance and place on the table and cover with tissue or plastic.

The simple folds are recommended for larger functions, while the more intricate designs are reserved for smaller, more intimate affairs. The space available on the table also determines the type of napkin fold you can use, especially for a buffet.

You will need to experiment with different size napkins in order to determine which folds are appropriate for the different size linens. Dinner napkins are usually about 22 inches square, and breakfast, luncheon, tea and cocktail napkins vary from 18 inches to smaller. Square linens are much easier to fold.

You can place your folded napkins to the left, right, center, above or on the plate, as well as in a glass. We have featured five folds on the following pages, including sculptured, flat, goblet and service designs, to encourage you to add folded napkins to your table.

You will find it considerably easier to fold napkins than it may first appear from looking at these illustrations. Do not hesitate to experiment. Folded napkins and hand-lettered place cards enhance every table setting, formal or informal, and demonstrate your flare for creative entertaining.

Bishop's Hat

1. Fold in half.

2. Fold left and right points to bottom point.

3. Fold top corner to 1" of bottom corner.

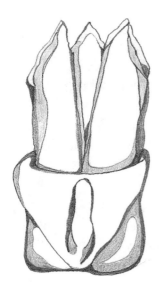

4. Fold corner back to edge.

5. Turn right side up.

6. Fold back sides and tuck in back.

Turn down two peaks of hat to make FLEUR DE LIS.

Standing Fan

1. Fold
in
half.

2. Fold in 1"
accordian
pleats up
to 4"
from top.

3. Fold in half.

4. Fold right corner
down and tuck in.

Place in the center,
or to the side, of
the plate.

Ascot Tie

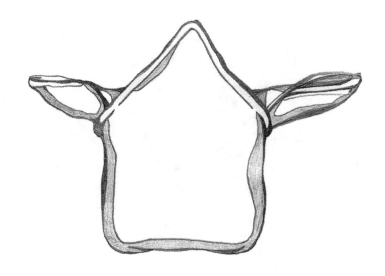

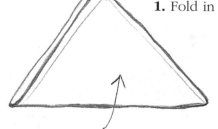

1. Fold in half.

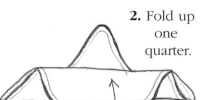

2. Fold up one quarter.

3. And again one quarter.

4. Fold sides over.

5. Turn over.

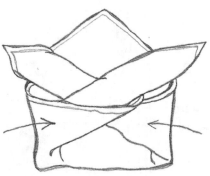

Special Buffet Server

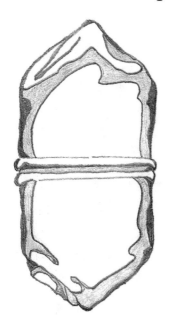

1. Fold corners to center.

2. Fold right half under.

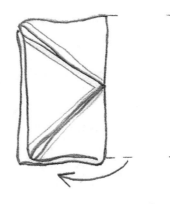

3. Fold bottom half under.

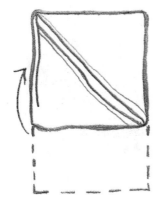

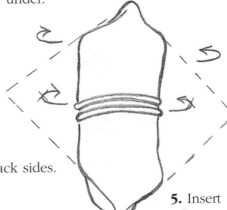

4. Fold back sides.

5. Insert flatware.

Rose

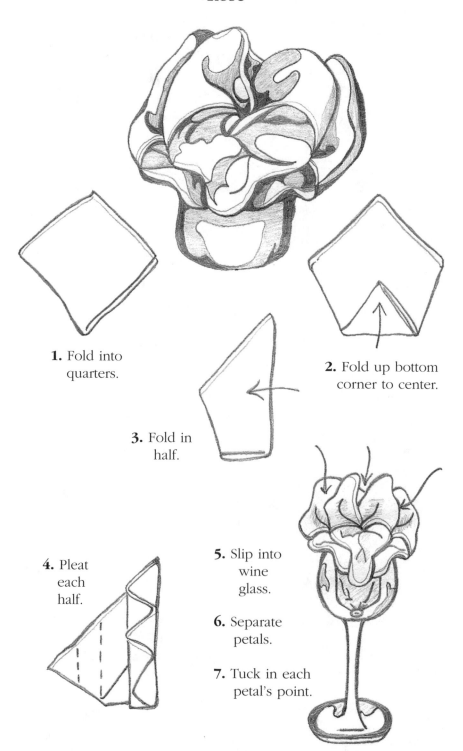

1. Fold into quarters.

2. Fold up bottom corner to center.

3. Fold in half.

4. Pleat each half.

5. Slip into wine glass.

6. Separate petals.

7. Tuck in each petal's point.

Sterling Silver

The standard place setting of silver flatware consists of five pieces, but etiquette still determines where it should be placed on the table. As stated in the introduction, we encourage you to use pieces in ways other than for what they were originally intended.

| Salad
Fork | Dinner
Fork | Dinner
Knife | Dessert
Spoon | Teaspoon |

At the turn of the century, the standard place setting consisted of twenty-five different forks, knives and spoons, with each piece of silver designated for a specific use. Strict etiquette of the period dictated the time of day and type of affair for which the silver was used, as well as where it should be placed on the table. The ornate designs and highly specialized serving pieces of the Victorian era have not since been duplicated.

| Bouillon Spoon | Fruit Spoon | Teaspoon | Ice Cream Spoon | Demitasse Spoon | Tablespoon | Iced Tea Spoon | Sauce Spoon | Cream Soup Spoon |

| Seafood Fork | Snail Fork | Pastry Fork | Dessert Fork | Salad Fork | Fish Fork | Luncheon Fork | Dinner Fork |

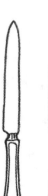    

| Fruit Knife | Steak Knife | Fish Knife | Butter Knife | Cheese Knife | Luncheon Knife | Dinner Knife |

Silver Care

Sometimes place settings are more interesting if you mix and match, so use and enjoy all of your silver regularly. It really does get more beautiful with constant use! Over time and with use, tiny microscopic lines will warm and mellow the surface of your sterling, resulting in a lustrous finish, or "patina."

Old monograms are wonderfully decorative. Do not remove them. Be creative and say that they belonged to great aunt xyz.

Wash immediately after each use with warm, soapy water, and dry thoroughly with a soft cloth. If unable to wash immediately, at least rinse in a sink or pan of warm, soapy water to remove the salt, eggs, mayonnaise, vinegar, fruits and/or vegetables that contain minerals and acids that can cause loss of color.

Your silver should be polished at least once or twice a year, whether it has been used regularly or not. It should never be dipped in cleaning solutions. That wonderful patina which has developed over the years can be removed in an instant! Instead, use a good paste or liquid cleaner and some "elbow grease."

Silver should never be lacquered. Part of the beauty of sterling silver is its lovely, soft sheen.

To store your silver, make sure that it is completely dry and do not use rubber bands, plastic wrap or newspaper. Store flat silver in proper cloths. Leave large decorative pieces out and enjoy as accessories.

By following these simple guidelines, your *Sterling Service* will remain a beautiful asset for years to come.

Index

- Index -

Sterling Service

Dothan Service League, P.O. Box 223, Dothan, Alabama 36302
334-671-7142

Please send _____ copies of Sterling Service at $19.95 each _____
Alabama residents add 8% ($1.60) tax _____
Add postage, handling and insurance at $3.50 each _____
Total _____

Circle one: Check   Visa   MasterCard

Card Number _____ Expiration Date _____

Signature _____

Make checks payable to: Dothan Service League
Ship to: (please print)

Name _____

Address _____

City _____ State _____ Zip _____

All proceeds from the sale of Sterling Service will be used
to support community projects of the Dothan Service League.

· · · · · · · · · · · · · · · · · · · cut here · · · · · · · · · · · · · · · · · · ·

Sterling Service

Dothan Service League, P.O. Box 223, Dothan, Alabama 36302
334-671-7142

Please send _____ copies of Sterling Service at $19.95 each _____
Alabama residents add 8% ($1.60) tax _____
Add postage, handling and insurance at $3.50 each _____
Total _____

Circle one: Check   Visa   MasterCard

Card Number _____ Expiration Date _____

Signature _____

Make checks payable to: Dothan Service League
Ship to: (please print)

Name _____

Address _____

City _____ State _____ Zip _____

All proceeds from the sale of Sterling Service will be used
to support community projects of the Dothan Service League.

If you would like to see *Sterling Service* carried in your area, please send us names and addresses of bookstores and/or gift shops. THANK YOU!

_____

_____

_____

_____

_____

_____

_____

· cut here ·

If you would like to see *Sterling Service* carried in your area, please send us names and addresses of bookstores and/or gift shops. THANK YOU!

_____

_____

_____

_____

_____

_____

_____